CCCC Studies in Writing & Rhetoric

FIRST SEMESTER

FIRST SEMESTER

GRADUATE STUDENTS, TEACHING WRITING, AND THE CHALLENGE OF MIDDLE GROUND

Jessica Restaino

Southern Illinois University Press
Carbondale and Edwardsville

Copyright © 2012 by the Conference on College Composition and Communication of the National Council of Teachers of English

All rights reserved

Printed in the United States of America

Publication partially funded by a subvention grant from the Conference on College Composition and Communication of the National Council of Teachers of English.

Library of Congress Cataloging-in-Publication Data
Restaino, Jessica, 1976–
First semester : graduate students, teaching writing, and the challenge of middle ground / Jessica Restaino.
    p. cm. — (Studies in writing & rhetoric)
Includes bibliographical references and index.
ISBN-13: 978-0-8093-3081-2 (pbk. : alk. paper)
ISBN-10: 0-8093-3081-4 (pbk. : alk. paper)
    1. English language—Rhetoric—Study and teaching. 2. English teachers—Training of. I. Title.
PE1404.R443 2012
808'.0420711—dc23   2011020636

The paper used in this publication meets the minimum requirements of American National Standard for Information Sciences—Permanence of Paper for Printed Library Materials, ANSI Z39.48-1992. ♾

For my daughters,
Abby and Thalia

I have a feeling of futility in everything I do. . . . I know this feeling disappears when I let myself fall into that gap between past and future which is the proper temporal locus of thought. Which I can't do when I am teaching and have to be all there.

—Hannah Arendt, in a letter to
Mary McCarthy, 9 February 1968

CONTENTS

ACKNOWLEDGMENTS

THIS BOOK CAME TO BE over a period of several years, and, as such, it has grown from the influence of many along the way. I have found myself surrounded by countless smart, resourceful, funny, inquisitive, and nurturing people, without whom this book could not—ever—have been written. While it is impossible to stuff all my gratitude into a few paragraphs, I hope I can at least make a dent.

The final version of this manuscript is a product of many drafts, for which I received excellent critical commentary from dedicated, astute readers. I want to thank Studies in Writing & Rhetoric reviewers Bianca Falbo and Stephen Ruffus for their careful attention, good questions, and intellectual rigor throughout this process, from proposal through final manuscript. Special thanks also go to Kristine Priddy at Southern Illinois University Press for her careful work with this manuscript in its later versions. Friend and former Montclair State University colleague Paul Butler held my hand as I slashed what was once the "methods" chapter; his comments were invaluable in helping me to craft an opening framework. Melissa Stein—stellar friend and trusted writing buddy—read every chapter, some multiple times, and has not wavered in her honesty and helpfulness. My thanks also go to friends and colleagues at Montclair State for their support, especially Lee Behlman for the many writing sessions and Emily Klein for pointing me in the direction of Christopher Higgins's work on Arendt. Finally, this book would not "be" without SWR editor Joseph Harris, who saw something here from the beginning and who gave me the chance to figure it out. I have learned endlessly from Joe's careful reading, vast knowledge, steady professionalism, and good nature.

I continue to benefit from the brilliance of excellent teachers. I owe much gratitude to Dean Hammer for first hooking me on Arendt's thought with his impassioned teaching. Padmini Mongia nurtured my sense of what is possible, personally and professionally, and still does. Fred Antczak saw potential in this project in its infancy and remains a giving mentor. Jerome Kohn shared his relationship with the real person, Hannah Arendt, and his unmatched knowledge of her work. Lisa Ede talked me through, after many emails, the theory/practice divide and told me to keep writing. Stephen Parks convinced me to stay in grad school after my own first semester and even drummed up generous support for my research from the Institute for the Study of Literature, Literacy, and Culture. Susan Wells's brilliance, encouragement, and excellent writing advice ("Claim the space!") fed the earliest manifestations of this project and continue to inspire me. And last but never least, Eli Goldblatt's steadfastness and openness as a teacher and scholar set the bar for me every day. I hope only to come close.

I am always learning how to teach writing, and I owe special thanks to those who have been in the throes of it with me as I've questioned and experimented. I would like to thank the study participants, who endured more of my musings than most and generously shared their own practices. Special thanks also go to Jaime Lynn Longo and April Logan for being great collaborators on the journey into teaching. Dennis Lebofsky and Michael Donnelly encouraged, cheered, and—when necessary—looked the other way as I found my own footing as a graduate student teacher at Temple. Emily Isaacs, my colleague at Montclair State University, welcomed my questions and shared her perspective as a writing program administrator. And, though impossible to name, my students teach me something new, inspire me to do better, and ignite my interests every time I enter a classroom.

Life did not stop for this book, and I owe my deepest thanks to those who live it with me each day. My parents, Carmen and Cheryl Restaino, have never wavered in their support and lovingly expanded our childcare reserves so I had additional time to write. My brilliant brother, Marc Restaino, is an endless source of wit, nourishing meals, and good laughs that have kept me human enough to stay with this work. Ryan Kline—husband, parenting partner, truest friend—is the energy behind anything I am able to accomplish, personally or professionally. And my daughters, Abby and Thalia, each born at some point during the long development of this project, have interrupted my writing more times than I can count to remind me that, really, books are not more important than playing. I thank them for the truth of this message and for letting me write anyway.

FIRST SEMESTER

1

Arendt, Writing Teachers, and Beginnings

AS HANNAH ARENDT POINTS OUT in her 1973 speech to the American Society of Christian Ethics, to start writing is a difficult—and sometimes arbitrary—task:

> I believe in this business, that to act is to begin. And I want to stress there, also, the difficulty, namely, that all beginning, as every one of you know who ever wrote a paper, has an element of utter arbitrariness. You know the enormous difficulty each one of us has to write the first sentence. And this element of arbitrariness, we should never forget. But at the same time, this arbitrariness is somehow a mirror of the fact of natality. You know if you try to think of your own birth in terms of this, that everything that is meaningful must be necessary. That is an old notion of philosophy: that only that which cannot not be, is meaningful. ("Remarks" 7)

This book project insists that, for new graduate students, to start teaching writing is a far more complex challenge. The blank page awaits the writer's first sentence, while new teachers, charged with the task of getting students to write and navigating new graduate programs themselves, are largely untrained, unsure of their responsibilities, and equipped with a syllabus they did not design and perhaps a list of pedagogical procedures they do not understand. The first semester is more of a day-to-day keeping afloat than it is a carefully constructed, planned course. My intention in this book is to isolate new graduate students' first semester as writing teachers for its drama, its real challenge to survival skills and adaptation, and its relevance as a shaky foundation on which writing programs and even scholarship rest. Arendt's ideas about beginnings, about necessity, and about work open meaningful angles from which to think through and question this drama.

During their first semester as writing instructors at "Public U," a large state university, I followed four brand-new graduate students and collected a range of ethnographic data. Two of the four were creative writers pursuing master's degrees in fiction; two were PhD students in English. Awarded prestigious "teaching assistantships," the four graduate students were each assigned to teach two sections of "English 50," the standard composition class required by Public U's First-Year Writing Program (FYWP), in exchange for full tuition reimbursement, a yearly stipend, and money for books each semester. They would have to learn how to be writing teachers while they also learned how to be graduate students. Among the four of them, they would have an audience of about two hundred students for their teaching debut.

While significant work exists on the preparation of new writing teachers—on topics ranging from mentoring programs to practicum courses—I want to argue that much of this work does not theorize the early experience of graduate students as writing teachers and its potential shaping of graduate students' understanding of composition as a discipline, nor the relationship between how writing instruction has been theorized and how it is practiced in the classroom.[1] I use the term "theorize" with caution here, resistant to notions of theory as an overly generalized explanation for a range of events and actions. Such approaches to theory rarely transfer seamlessly across local contexts and can be more limiting than enlightening. Instead, I approach the theorizing of graduate students' first semester teaching experience mindful of Adrienne Rich's warning—echoed by Lisa Ede—about the perils of dislocated theory: "But if it doesn't smell of the earth, it isn't good for the earth" (qtd. in Ede, *Situating Composition* 155). This project applies frameworks for thinking about what happened in four graduate students' first writing classrooms. This interaction between theory and practice is not about making sweeping conclusions but rather an effort to understand questions and possibilities relevant to one local context that may, ultimately, raise new questions and possibilities when applied to other teaching contexts. As Joseph Harris has written on the uses of theory, "Ideas are usually interesting precisely to the degree that they are meant to have practical consequences" ("Rhetoric" 147). My intention is that the ideas explored in this book will provide new pathways to critical and expanded practice.

THE SITE: LOCATION AND PROGRAM

Public U is located in an urban northeastern US city and can be described as an ethnically and racially diverse institution. Though there has been a recent influx in students from the surrounding suburbs, Public U maintains ties to city public schools and also draws a portion of its student body from the nontraditional, working adult population. Most undergraduates are required to pass English 50, the standard college composition course offered by the FYWP. Students whose writing is assessed as more remedial are required to take two semesters of composition, beginning with English 40 and moving on to 50. The FYWP also offers two sections of composition for English language learners, English 41 and 51.

The FYWP at Public U serves more undergraduate students than any other department in the university and also employs more teachers. At the time of this study, graduate students awarded teaching assistantships were required to teach two courses per semester; immediately following my data collection semester, the load was changed to two courses in the fall and one in the spring. Most English 50 classes are capped at twenty-two students, but class lists can easily reach twenty-five. For a graduate student teaching in the FYWP, a semester with a two-course load involves teaching about fifty undergraduates, no small task when grading papers and managing one's graduate coursework is considered.

First-year teaching assistants (TAs) are introduced to the FYWP and their new jobs at a three-day orientation prior to the start of the fall semester. At orientation, new teachers participate in workshops on grading and classroom management and are introduced to the syllabus they must teach during their first semester. While the FYWP allows teachers to develop their own syllabi in later semesters, all new teachers are required to follow a set syllabus during their first semester at Public U. Additionally, new TAs must take a graduate level course, the teaching practicum, taught by an English department faculty member with expertise in composition. During the semester of my research, the practicum professor was a full-time, tenure-track faculty member with expertise in composition but was not the FYWP administrator. Traditionally, students meet the practicum professor during orientation and receive an introduction to the course. New teachers, organized into small groups, are also assigned mentors, advanced graduate students with considerable teaching experience. Throughout the semester, mentors are required to hold regular meetings, observe the new teachers, and assess their grading. They are also asked to serve as a resource for the new teachers, offering advice and assistance when necessary.

During the semester of my data collection, new graduate students taught English 50 via an assigned syllabus of the practicum professor's design. The course emphasized class struggle and the politics of location, including issues relevant to the surrounding community. Readings included work by Chinua Achebe, Raymond Williams, Antonio Gramsci, and Mary Louise Pratt and a collection of community writing. Additionally, first-year writing students were required to submit five essays, completed through a series of drafts and revisions, and to participate in several conferences with the instructor. Students also were required to turn in a portfolio of their revised work at the end of the semester for final review.

METHODS OF DATA COLLECTION

I recruited the four participants for this study via a letter I sent out during the summer before their first semester at Public U (see appendix A). Four was the maximum number of participants I felt I could work with, as I hoped to develop a substantial, interactive relationship with each participant. The graduate students in this book were collaborators in my research: they generously granted me permission to quote them, observe their classes, study their grading practices, talk with them at great length, and generally hang around them as they found their way during their first semester teaching experiences. In response, they shared with me—in discussion and in writing—their goals, fears, frustrations, and questions as new writing teachers.

After initial introductory emails and phone conversations, data collection began during the required FYWP orientation in late August. I also attended parts of the orientation in order to introduce myself and get a sense of the administration's approach for the semester. I had participants fill out a survey detailing their perceptions of the orientation and their sense of what was expected of them as writing teachers, and I also invited them to use the back of the survey to "rant" about their concerns and worries as the semester approached (see appendix B for a copy of the survey). In early September, I began our monthly "happy hour": the five of us regularly met at the campus bar for drinks and discussion. I always brought my tape recorder to these events and usually had some particular direction crafted beforehand, though our conversations were unpredictable and open.

Throughout the semester, I visited classrooms and also observed numerous student/teacher conferences. The FYWP required at least three conferences per student each semester. New teachers must learn how to talk about writing in instructive ways, and they also must learn how to listen to students in these sessions. The listening is always the hardest, and many new teachers struggle with this skill. I maintained detailed notes during classroom observations and student conferences.

I also collected at least two batches of student papers from each participant. I was most interested in studying the marginal and end comments from the teachers, as well as in assessing their grading scales. I looked at papers that the teachers graded early in the semester and also at a batch graded in the last weeks. It was particularly interesting to note the development in commentary; often it evolved from grammar pointers to instructive support on developing argument and critical thought. Participants and I were in regular dialogue about the evolution of their assessments of and responses to student writing.

I visited the required teaching practicum course a couple of times during the semester to get a sense of the class climate. The new teachers had to write short responses to a selection of readings, which included scholarship by Nancy Sommers, David Bartholomae, Sondra Perl, Lisa Delpit, and Glynda Hull. I collected participants' responses, particularly when the topic was controversial in the field. The graduate students were also required to complete a final project for the course that included a short research paper on an area of interest in the teaching of composition, a newly designed syllabus that built on this interest, a statement of teaching philosophy, and three graded student writing samples, complete with a one-page written exploration of each. I also collected these projects from each participant. We often discussed the practicum during our happy hour sessions, as some participants found the course to be extra work rather than a support system for their teaching, despite the details of the final project. The description of the course as a "teaching practicum" tends to convince many new teachers that the class is only a supportive teaching workshop where they can brainstorm teaching ideas and talk about classroom management. However, the course additionally attempts to provide new teachers with at least a basic foundation in theories of composing and pedagogy. Graduate students, attending Public U to pursue creative writing or a doctorate in literature, often resent the work this course demands.

Perhaps the most significant data was collected via correspondence I had with participants. I learned very quickly that I would gain access to far richer data if I became a useful—rather than a merely observant—presence for the new teachers. So, instead of always posing as a researcher who needed information from them, I assured them that every interaction between us was "data" and that they should feel free to consult me as a resource. I quickly became a participant-observer, engulfed in their experiences and called upon regularly regarding various emergencies, problem students, emotional outbursts, and so on. Although I shared numerous phone conversations with participants, most communication was via email. By the end of the semester, I compiled a master document of email correspondence that totaled over one hundred pages of text. At least every couple of days I received emails detailing struggles, asking for advice, or just ranting about various frustrations and insecurities. I have had to wrestle with the challenges this role as participant-observer posed to my study and revisit them as necessary throughout the book. However, my quick transition to this role was crucial because, quite frankly, if I was not going to be useful to the new teachers, they really would not have had much time for my study. Furthermore, the quality of the data I gathered was directly connected to my relationship with the participants. Because I became someone they trusted and relied upon, I was invited into their experiences as a friend and mentor. Formality was washed away, and raw experience was left behind. The fact of the "study" was often forgotten.

At the end of the semester, I participated in the portfolio reviews required by the FYWP. We worked together as a group of five, and I served as facilitator for the review. Teachers had to read the portfolios of each other's students and assess them as "high pass," "pass," and "fail." They also had to present to each other student portfolios that represented each grade level (A, B, C) in order to confirm the accuracy of their grading scales. I recorded reflective notes from the seven-hour portfolio review and served as "tie breaker" when participants had disagreements about portfolios. Throughout the day following our portfolio review, I conducted exit interviews with each participant. In these interviews, I sat down one-on-one with each of them and just turned on the tape recorder. I invited them to recap and reflect on their first semester. During these interviews, I worked hard to speak minimally, although my relationship with the participants was very interactive by this point. The exit interviews were immensely valuable to my study, and my examination of the transcripts revealed the distinctions and richness of each participant.

THE PARTICIPANTS

In what follows, I offer descriptions of the four graduate students in this study. I have written these descriptions in collaboration with the study participants themselves; I leaned heavily on these graduate students for decisions regarding the personal attributes they felt most important for readers to know about them. All details included below that designate "who" each participant is—including the selection of pseudonyms—come at the participant's request and direction. The graduate students in this study also wrote descriptions about their feelings, questions, and anxieties about teaching writing both before and after their summer TA orientation. When possible, I have quoted this writing directly and at some length. My intention here is to stress that study participants operated as meaningful, co-collaborators for the duration of my data collection and beyond.[2] While I take sole responsibility for the analysis that follows, I have found myself to be, throughout my work on this book, their constant, indebted student.

Shirley

An African American woman in her late twenties, Shirley came to Public U's English department to study fiction and get her master's degree in creative writing. Before enrolling, Shirley worked as a paralegal; the job left its mark in Shirley's careful attention to detail, spotless appearance, and very composed demeanor. Immediately following new teacher orientation and prior to the start of the semester, Shirley's major concern was her lack of preparation. She felt that "those of us with no teaching experience have been tossed into the deep end" and resented the FYWP's failure to better prepare new teachers for the first day. She noted that by the second day of orientation, many new teachers still hadn't received the syllabus they were supposed to teach; when they did get hold of it, those who were teaching two days a week discovered the syllabus had been designed for courses that met Monday, Wednesday, and Friday. Shirley wrote in her "rant" section of the post-orientation survey:

> As a freshman, I had high ideals about college and college life, and professors who showed up and didn't seem to care—and to me, lack of preparation displayed lack of caring—frustrated me. I don't want to do that to my students. The whirlwind, last-minute orientation made me concerned that this may happen, regardless of my intentions. (post-orientation survey)

Shirley's teaching persona early on in the semester was all business; she consistently paired this demeanor with a professional appearance, complete with "bunned" hair. She attributed this style to her "short woman complex," citing often that due to her youthful face, gender, and small stature, she felt it important to reinforce her authority via seriousness and a professional presence. She would later admit, too, that her racial minority status was a source of extra pressure to "prove" herself, particularly in light of the fact that she had an overwhelming majority of white students in her two courses. Shirley was her own toughest critic: she tended to set very high standards and push herself ambitiously. During our first happy hour session, Shirley boldly asserted that she was at Public U to work on her fiction, which would always come before teaching; she was not there to be a teacher. Shirley described her pre-semester attitude toward teaching: "Find a way to get through this with as little involvement as possible. Don't let anything about teaching get in the way of writing/studying. Make it through the next two years without screwing up too badly, pad the CV, and never do this again" (post-orientation survey). I admired her assertive stance, though also found it tinged at the time with more self-defense than real distaste for teaching. Regardless, I respectfully noted this position as a starting point for Shirley and anticipated an interesting semester experience for her.

Nancy

Twenty-three years old and Caucasian, Nancy was the youngest member of our group. She had graduated a year earlier from a prestigious West Coast university and came to Public U's doctoral program with a real interest in studying composition. This set her apart from the others, who had intentions of studying literature or creative writing when they arrived at Public U. She defined herself as a teacher first and admitted that she often questioned her enrollment in a doctoral program: "Half the time I think I should just become a high school teacher." She further admitted, however, that she somehow acquired the belief growing up that "teaching was beneath me" (exit interview).

Nancy was a quiet person who did not express her concerns or anxieties as openly as the others did. At the start of the semester, she felt underprepared to grade students' writing. In her post-orientation survey, she wrote: "We received handouts on grading, but we didn't really talk about it as a group. . . . I don't really feel, though, that I would know the difference between an A and a B paper." My analysis of her commentary on students' writing, however, would convince me that Nancy really had a natural eye for instructive feedback and a writer's development. Nancy increasingly defined herself as distinct from her fellow graduate students, claiming she felt more of a connection to her undergraduates and expressing her distaste for her peers' tendency to complain about their workloads (exit interview).

Nancy's most distinguishing characteristic was this allegiance to her undergraduates, coupled with resentment toward her peers' complaints about students and their generally negative attitude toward the first-year course. Although she had not taught before, she did not feel especially threatened by the situation; she considered it, instead, her good fortune. On the "rant" section of her post-orientation survey, her main concern was that some discussion during orientation cast students "as enemies and . . . as antagonistic." She followed this up positively, however, with the conclusion that it was valuable to later speak to the faculty member teaching the practicum course "because he talked about how fun and intelligent the students can be" (post-orientation survey). All in all, Nancy did not present herself as thoroughly overwhelmed or uncomfortable with her situation. She also demonstrated an eagerness and optimism about the students she would teach and the discipline of composition.

Anjel

The only male participant in the study, Anjel was openly gay, Asian American, and twenty-nine years old. He also had graduated from a prestigious West Coast university; afterward, he went on to work in corporate America before deciding to attend graduate school. He came to Public U to study fiction and receive his master's degree in creative writing. Anjel had never taught writing before, although he did teach conversational English in Vietnam for two years. Anjel's attitude at the start of the semester was generally relaxed; from early on he claimed he did not feel very nervous about teaching. He had a natural classroom presence, and his first semester at Public U would not be his first standing before students. He offered thoughtful insight into his confidence: "Chalk it up to age again or maybe being gay, but I have complete confidence in my public persona. I've had time to develop a confident public persona, am used to wearing a public persona, and am comfortable (at least superficially) in my own skin" (email, 14 Jan.). Furthermore, Anjel's experience teaching in Vietnam prepared him, more than the other participants in the study, for administrative glitches, work overloads, and the challenge of thinking on his feet:

> I taught overseas for 2 years, and I knew if I could handle a class of 100 kids who didn't speak my language, I could handle 23 Americans—no matter how bad they could be. Also, Viet Nam was all about confusion and contradictory teaching assignments and heavy teaching loads. So I was very used to improvising in class, having a classroom in flux, coming up with a syllabus the night before an 8AM class, and thinking I had NO idea what was going on. All that made teaching my first semester at Public U much easier. (exit interview)

Anjel's classroom confidence could not, however, calm his suspicion that his teaching load would compromise his graduate studies. He expressed disappointment following orientation that the FYWP did not make at least the administrative work easier for the new teachers, particularly given their other responsibilities in adjusting to grad school. He wrote in his post-orientation questionnaire:

> I'd feel a LOT better about managing my time if FYWP stepped up to the plate by giving us complete and copied syllabi, course readers, and complete lesson plans. Why bother with the pretense that we're teaching autonomous courses anyway? We all teach the same syllabus, same readings, take the same practicum. And why does the practicum sound like a lot of work? I didn't sign up for graduate school in creative writing to study comp/rhetoric! Yes, a course supporting TAs is fine, but no, that course shouldn't involve almost $100 in books I'll never use again or a "writing intensive research paper."

The apprehension Anjel shared in his post-orientation questionnaire is not unusual for new graduate students hired to teach writing. Many, if not most, do not plan on careers in the field and so are easily stressed by the idea that the practicum may add extra work to their graduate pursuits.

Anjel approached the task of teaching with an attitude that differed from the norm: he was rarely overwhelmed and did not constantly question his own authority. The influence of gender on approaches to the first-year writing classroom seemed a relevant, potential factor in Anjel's experience, as compared to the other three participants.[3] He consistently came up with strategies that protected him from being overrun by the workload and preserved time for his own studies. At one point, he set a timer to limit his work on each graded paper. He later gave up this experiment, deciding it was too structured, but he regularly approached his teaching responsibilities committed equally to preserving his sanity and time for his own writing and to the students he had to teach. Anjel also regularly partner-taught with Shirley; the two would swap lessons or co-plan lessons so as to help lighten each other's loads. Additionally, despite his initial resentment toward the practicum course, Anjel became a student of his own pedagogical development: he experimented with different approaches, learned from his students, and was consistently reflective. He appeared to be very much steering the course of his first semester experience, despite teaching a required syllabus not of his design.

Tess

The teacher who would weather the most tempestuous semester, Tess was a Caucasian woman in her mid-twenties. She had graduated from Public U with a bachelor's degree in English and worked for a nonprofit educational organization immediately following graduation; she then returned to Public U to pursue a PhD in literature. Her previous experience with the university helped her to anticipate and maneuver bureaucratic issues; in fact, she chose to participate in my study because she knew it would give her some connection, or community, at a large school where it is easy to get lost. She believed that a support system would be essential to her first semester. Tess's connection to Public U was also significant because she was the only participant in the study who had taken English 50 as a student. Accordingly, she taught the class with a different level of insight from the others.

Tess's greatest concern immediately after the orientation was time management. On her post-orientation survey, she asked, "How do I write papers and grade papers???" She then expanded:

> I don't think there are hours in the day, days in the week, weeks in the semester to accomplish everything in a meticulous way. I am a meticulous person; it bothers me that I will have to compromise my standards because of time constraints. I almost feel that with a workload of teach-2-classes, take-3-classes each semester, I am being set up to fail. If not to fail, then to wind up having to do things "half-assed." I'm not comfortable with that. I am committed to educating students about writing (which is, I believe, the most important skill anyone can learn and master), and I am also committed to my own studies. How do I do all this and maintain my own sanity? Seriously!

It is important to note that Tess's concerns here were personality-related. She put a lot of pressure on herself to do well, was an ambitious person, and began the semester with a real sense of responsibility toward the two classes of students she would teach. Her initial apprehensions reminded me of Shirley's: both shared significant concern about disappointing or short-changing students. Their conscientiousness caused them to be regularly self-reflective, which proved an invaluable benefit to my research. Tess took me along throughout the semester on her own self-investigations as she learned to teach and manage the trials that came her way. She questioned herself, she openly expressed frustration, and she noticed when improvements had been made or milestones reached. She also noted moments when she sensed real professional growth in herself as a teacher.

Unfortunately, during the semester Tess was confronted with an emotionally and psychologically troubled male student. This situation will be discussed at length in chapter 3. For now, though, it is necessary to say that this struggle diverted her experience sharply at one point in the semester. Up until this confrontation, Tess was discovering herself and her interests as a writing teacher. Afterward, she would have to struggle to stay focused and to reconnect with her love for teaching and interest in composition as a field. I was privileged to be a confidant at this time and have attempted, as a researcher, to make sense of this incident as thoughtfully as possible. By the end of the semester, Tess's experiences would push the limits of Arendtian analysis and make a convincing, important case for teaching's capacity for personal investment and emotional hardship.

BUILDING BRIDGES: ARENDT AS LENS FOR READING PRACTICE

I arrived at this work with dual interests: the struggle of new writing teachers and the political theory of Hannah Arendt. When I started to work with Arendt's three-part theoretical construct of labor, work, and action, which she establishes most fully in her 1958 work *The Human Condition*, as a model for studying new writing teachers, I had to confront the interdependence, balance, and, at times, interchangeability of these three concepts. They are in orbit with each other. Each offers ways of thinking about writing instruction, the writing classroom, and teacher development. However, as soon as we begin to match theoretical pieces to real-life teachers, the delicate tensions amid the concepts intervene to underscore the unpredictability, distinctiveness, and play within and among writing teachers themselves. In other words, there is nothing simple about learning how to teach writing, and there is nothing simple to say about writing teachers. From my efforts to apply Arendtian analysis, I learned, first, that I cannot put real people and real situations into neat categories.

In *The Human Condition*, Arendt likens labor (which is the focus of the following chapter) to "tilled soil," which, "if it is to remain cultivated, needs to be labored upon time and again" (157). Laboring is never finished; it is the giant task of staying alive. At the end of each day, our labor is wiped away, and we are faced with yet another weedy garden. My own approach to this concept, initially, was to ask a series of questions. First, what does "staying alive" look like for the new writing teacher? In other words, what is the work of sustenance in a new teacher's first writing classroom? Could it be the writing process itself or the task of having something to do each day with twenty-something students? Or, could laboring for the new teacher be classroom management, tending to the differing personalities and learning styles of students, without ever feeling a sense of security and authority before the class? Might grading operate as labor, a kind of sustenance, the new teacher's only means of maintaining this shaky authority?

If labor is an endless and repetitious cycle, Arendt's concepts of action and work (which share the focus of chapter 3) serve as mediating forces that, through their very reliance on each other, interrupt labor's course of otherwise natural decay. Arendt explains that the "life span of man running toward death would inevitably carry everything human to ruin and destruction if it were not for the faculty of interrupting it and beginning something new" (*Human Condition* 246). Action is thus represented by the moments of brilliance that happen despite, or in the course of, our daily lives. These moments are also public ones; they occur for others to see. In fact, Arendt often describes action as a self-disclosure or revelation, where we appear as ourselves before others. For this reason, Arendt connects action to "plurality" because action is utterly dependent upon the presence of others to witness and remember. In terms of new writing teachers, there are countless circumstances that seem potentially stifling—their unpreparedness, their heavy workload, university expectations for what the course should look like—and I anticipated, in the context of this study, that the study participants would be consumed by mere survival rather than spurred to invention and interruption. Still, exactly such stifling conditions can also be the impetus for change. I approached data collection with a number of questions about action, were it to happen at all for the teachers I was studying. First, where might action happen for new writing teachers? Does action happen in front of the classroom? In marginal comments on papers, conversing with students? In student conferences? With university administrators and colleagues?

Or, would it happen during the hours spent in the English department's required teaching practicum course, among fellow new writing teachers? If action was not possible, what were the consequences of teaching without it?

Extending our understanding of the possibilities of action, in chapter 3, work—or "fabrication"—is the lasting record, made by human hands, of our most striking words and deeds. Work is the product, or proof, of human ingenuity, rebellion, and resistance. Arendt explains in *The Human Condition* that "the doing of great deeds and the speaking of great words will leave no trace, no product that might endure after the moment of action and the spoken word has passed" (173). Such words and deeds are saved with the "help of the artist, of poets and historiographers, of monument-builders or writers, because without them . . . the story they enact and tell, would not survive at all" (173). In my approach to studying new teachers in their first semester, I tried to consider a broad spectrum in defining classroom product. What is the fabrication of the new writing teacher? Is it the grade book? The students who have passed first-year composition? Or, is it the teacher's written commentary in the margins of student papers, the evidence of a budding instructive role? Is the work of the new writing teacher his or her first syllabus or assignments? (But what if they are not his own but preformulated ones the teacher must teach, assign, and grade?) Further—and perhaps most important—what can we learn about how graduate students learn to teach writing by looking at these classroom products?

My role as researcher and writer speaks to the complex overlaps in Arendt's thought and its value as a lens for understanding graduate students' first teaching semester. Ultimately, in exploring the interplay between these concepts, I came to value a middle space for graduate students, where they can experiment safely on the border between work and action while also safeguarding themselves from labor's consumptive grasp. The new teachers in my study were often in the grips of the necessity-type demands of getting through each class and also struggled against these demands at times. I was at once responding to these needs and struggles and also charting them for the sake of documentation and storytelling. Similarly, then, in my own efforts I discovered my location betwixt and between Arendt's major concepts. My interest was as much fabrication as it was seeing that the new teachers stayed afloat. Publication of this study is also at the crossroads of Arendtian action and work: the teachers' experiences in this study need an audience if they stand to disrupt the normal course of teacher preparation, the mentoring of new graduate students, and the ways in which we value new teachers' contributions. In the final chapter in this book, I explore the possibilities for how, as a field, we can work collaboratively to achieve these goals given the complex positioning of composition in the university.

My role as "speaker" on behalf of the graduate students in this study and the extent to which my storytelling represents their experiences in potentially limited or narrowly perceived ways, particularly as I apply Arendtian analysis, remain ongoing quandaries for this book.[4] Arendt's discussion of the worker's role in recording powerful moments of speech and action does little to shed light on the possible hierarchies involved. While I attempt to let the teachers in this book speak for themselves as much as possible, I ultimately offer one way of reading what they experienced. From my perspective, Arendt's theoretical framework is valuable because the pieces are in flux: each must not overwhelm the others if the health of the "world" or "network of human relationships" is to stay in check. I find that thinking through this model, particularly in light of this threat, becomes a way of assigning meaning to the many facets of graduate students' first formulations of teaching practice and, I hope, highlights the kinds of questions we should ask and the ways in which we may need to disrupt the course in our varied local contexts. However, I also maintain that the graduate students in this study are not meant to represent a kind of generalized example for the field, nor should Arendt's theoretical construct serve as a frame for reading graduate students' experiences devoid of the particularities of their local contexts.

The stories in this book are built from ethnographic, qualitative data, which draw on a range of methods. In the end, the best stories we tell are the ones that connect us to each other. In his essay "The

Narrative Roots of Case Study," Thomas Newkirk insists that "the strength of this mode of research is not in producing generalizable conclusions, guaranteed by rigorous and objective observation procedures" (132). Rather, he argues, in case study research we "are made to feel that we are face-to-face with Reality itself, detailed, alive, recognizable" (133). While I would not categorize this book as a collection of case studies, I hope that the range of experiences shared by graduate students here is recognizable to many and thus opens various contexts to Arendtian questions.

SITUATING THE PROJECT: ARENDT, COMPOSITION, AND TEACHER PREPARATION

Despite graduate students' crucial role in making writing programs work, there exist proportionally few efforts to study their experiences. Of the work that is extant, much of it is either outdated or highly practical, lacking consideration of the theoretical significance graduate students in the classroom pose to composition as a field. The earliest *College Composition and Communication* piece describing teacher preparation is Robert S. Hunting's "Training Course for Teachers of Freshman Composition," published in 1951. As early as 1963, *CCC* published a series, "Training Graduate Students as Teachers," which outlined early efforts to put graduate students in the writing classroom. The series features articles from writing program administrators (WPAs) at Penn State, Loyola University, Arizona State University, and the University of Illinois. The articles generally present "best practices," outlining newly implemented mentoring programs and introductory courses and reflecting on graduate students' struggles. John S. Bowman, writing on Penn State's usage of graduate student teachers, reflects on this familiar-sounding plight: "Sometimes the fledgling has been simply handed the course syllabus and wished well, perhaps with the promise of a look-in now and then by a professional member of the department" (73). Bowman's use of the pathetic term "fledgling" is echoed by James D. Barry's description of his grad students' adjustment to teaching at Loyola: "The extent to which I make them realize the stains on my jacket are traceable to the tears of last year's assistants, and that the space is available to absorb more of the same, controls the relationship that develops" (76). The "relationship that develops" is clearly a paternalistic one, defined by new teachers' inevitable, unfixable suffering. Casting graduate student teachers as travelers on a kind of disastrous rite of passage, these early accounts fail to imagine them as potential contributors to how writing gets taught and theorized. Additional "best practices" pieces surfaced in *CCC* in the late 1960s and again in the 1970s, such as Richard L. Larson's 1966 "Staffroom Interchange" piece, "Training New Teachers of Composition in the Writing of Comments on Themes," and Nancy S. Prichard's 1970 "The Training of Junior College English Teachers." Both speak practically to WPAs burdened with the task of training inexperienced teachers for the composition classroom.

While pieces on training new composition teachers would continue to surface, they would do so sporadically until Charles W. Bridges's 1986 compilation, *Training the New Teacher of College Composition*. Again, many of the essays feature best practices approaches to TA orientation, the teaching practicum, and mentoring. Taking perhaps the boldest position in the book, Maxine Hairston in "On Not Being a Composition Slave" outlines the pitfalls of overwork in the writing classroom to which new graduate students are most susceptible. In his review of the collection, Ken Davis tellingly identifies the status of teacher preparation issues in the field: "As pedagogical pieces become ever sparser in the journals in our field—crowded out by the renaissance of research and theory—these articles, too, fill a need." Davis's review points to an important and long-standing conceptual gap between teacher preparation and "research and theory." My book is an effort to close that gap and argues, instead, that the preparation of graduate students to teach writing is a significant focal point for theory, research, and practice. More recent collections on the subject of graduate student preparation seem to push toward the blurring of these boundaries, as well. Betty P. Pytlik and Sarah Liggett's *Preparing College Teachers of Writing: Histories, Theories, Programs, Practices* is a wide-ranging compilation of essays that includes a section on theoretical considerations and programs' philosophical orientations, as well as a more extensive historical review of teacher preparation than I offer here. In 2005, Sidney Dobrin edited *Don't Call It That: The Composition Practicum*, a collection of essays written primarily by WPAs that looks at the practicum course as an often conflicted, contested space where students' needs for practical tools clash with instructors' theoretical approaches to the course.

Interestingly, graduate students' voices are often unheard in much of this scholarship. Tina Lavonne Good and Leanne B. Warshauer's collection *In Our Own Voice: Graduate Students Teach Writing* marks a break in this silence. The encouraging response to their call for papers underscores the need for such work on graduate student teaching, as Good and Warshauer attest: "The response was overwhelming—from hundreds of people who submitted papers and paper proposals to well-wishers and writing program administrators in both two-year and four-year colleges and universities across the country" (x). Good and Warshauer share their hope that "the graduate-student voice [will be] recognized as authoritative and useful in the field of composition studies" (x). This challenge is echoed by Mary Lou Odom's 2004 dissertation, "Before the Classroom: Teachers Theorizing First-Year Composition Pedagogy." Odom uses case study accounts of teacher training to investigate graduate students' formation of theories of writing prior to their first experiences of classroom practice. Odom's work is most important in its effort to take seriously graduate students' contribution to our field's uses of theory and the problematic split between theory and practice. My book echoes the conviction that graduate students are authoritative and crucial participants in the teaching and theorizing of first-year writing.

Composition as a field has made few connections to the work of Hannah Arendt, though I do find some encouraging bridges. Toward the end of his work *A Teaching Subject: Composition since 1966*, Joseph Harris critiques the popular term "discourse community" and uses Arendt's notion of the "public" as an alternative. Harris argues, "What I find most interesting and useful about this notion of a public is that it refers not to a group of people (like a community) but to a kind of space and process, a point of contact that needs to be created and continuously maintained" (108). Only one year later, in 1998, Anne Ruggles Gere and Aaron Schutz published an article in *College English*, "Service Learning and English Studies: Rethinking 'Public' Service," which draws upon Arendt's notion of the public sphere to argue for the incorporation of service-learning efforts in the English classroom. They describe the idea of a "public" that is "focused on what Arendt sometimes calls 'the love of the world'; it is focused on the elaboration of the common project and the maintenance of a space in which individuals might 'appear' in some relative equality, taking positions around such a project" (141). This shared public is a unifying thread in Patricia Roberts-Miller's 2002 *Journal of Advanced Composition* piece, "Fighting without Hatred: Hannah Arendt's Agonistic Rhetoric." Roberts-Miller contends that Arendt is a theorist useful to negotiating a classroom space in which argument is not divisive but rather constructive. While I make somewhat different use of Arendt in this book, I find that the interlocking nature of her theoretical concepts serves as a kind of equation for discovering new revelations about relationships among teachers, institutions, programs, and students.

2

Labor and Endlessness: Necessity and Consumption in the First Semester

> The experience of studenthood is the experience of being just so
> far over one's head that it is both realistic and essential to work
> at surviving.
>
> —Mina Shaughnessy, *Errors and Expectations*

NEW GRADUATE STUDENTS in the composition classroom are, in addition to everything else, also students of teaching. At places like Public U, where they must teach during their first semester of graduate coursework, that semester is a scrambling, do-or-die kind of experience, complete with funding packages in the balance. These graduate students are usually barely (if at all) students of composition theory and must find a way to make it through. They may feel as if they are drowning, but with drive and perseverance they can come up for air eventually. Still, what are the consequences of this struggle for control? By the end of the first semester, graduate students may feel more confident about their teaching abilities. However, this confidence in no way suggests more than a cursory knowledge about how writing has been theorized, the field's major debates, or the history of composition's disciplinary development. Analysis of the struggle to survive in our first-year writing classrooms uncovers deep roots in the tensions between theory and practice. New teachers often learn to enact classroom practices without intellectual exploration of the theoretical rationale for those practices. This moment in early teaching may be one of the most poignant in our field's long tradition of disconnect between how writing is theorized and how it is taught by the many graduate students and adjuncts who predominantly staff first-year writing classrooms.

RUNNING IN THE WHEEL: ARENDT AND SURVIVAL

The Arendtian notion of labor is consumptive; it signifies those efforts that are immediately devoured as soon as they are enacted. In *The Human Condition*, Hannah Arendt likens laboring to tilled soil, which, "if it is to remain cultivated, needs to be labored upon time and again" (157). Accordingly, the role of laboring in Arendtian society is sustenance and necessity. We can think of labor as akin to biological process, in the sense that once is never good enough. The effort needs to be repeated "time and again" if life is to be sustained, much like eating or drinking. In fact, laboring is running in an endless wheel for the sake of the wheel itself; it is our everyday biological function, without which we could not do anything else. Arendt insists that life itself depends upon laboring; however, the laborer always has nothing to "show" for his or her efforts: "It is indeed the mark of all laboring that it leaves nothing behind, that the result of its effort is almost as quickly consumed as the effort is spent. And yet this effort, despite its futility, is born of a greater urgency and motivated by a more powerful drive than anything else, because life itself depends upon it" (87).

Clearly, Arendt defines an activity that is located at the metaphorical bottom of the societal pyramid: laboring is most essential, yet rewarded with the least enduring of gifts.[1] Parallels between Arendt's laborer and the first-year writing instructor are at once frightening, reasonable, and an intellectual stretch. On one hand, the requirement status typical of the course, graduate student instructors' sink-or-swim first-semester experience, and students' often overly eager consumption of draft comments in pursuit of a desirable grade all work toward this idea of quickly consumed and quickly erased efforts. However, it is also impossible to see the writing classroom as a space where efforts leave nothing behind. Certainly, there is much to "take" from the first-year writing classroom in the form of instruction, assessment, and developed skills for both students and teacher. However, these potential gains were often illusive and untenable to the new teachers in my study, precisely because of the ways in which their work mirrored laboring. Many of these rewards—including the benefits of actually studying new graduate student teachers—are tangible to (and even used by) others, like researchers, students, and WPAs. The challenge, then, is to explore the consequences—the "what if"—embedded in Arendt's notion of laboring. What happens if, in these early efforts to survive, to stay afloat, new teachers learn to teach writing in a way that undermines the potential for the enduring, lasting contributions of instruction, even to their own development as teachers? I will argue that this "what if" is a real danger for new graduate student writing teachers and its impact is felt across theory, practice, and discipline.

The "life itself depends on it" feel of that first semester has much to do with the fact that new teachers are often figuring out how to be teachers while, of course, teaching their first class(es). Accordingly, there is a fundamental level at which the new teacher must simply strive to create a legitimate class, one that students buy into, that actually runs from the beginning of the semester to the end. As Timothy R. Donovan, Patricia Sprouse, and Patricia Williams write of graduate student TAs, "Something happens in the classroom: They become teachers. They discover that there is more involved than imparting a codified body of knowledge, following a pack- aged lesson plan, or mimicking another teacher" (139). While such self-discovery and professional development may be at work during the first semester, it is easy for new teachers to find themselves quite removed from feelings of growth and self-determination. Student demands, particularly around grading, strike new teachers with an urgency that threatens the very core of their legitimacy. Accordingly, much of what new teachers do has an air of just keeping it together, proving themselves (to themselves as well as students). The task of just making the class real, from the new teacher's perspective, tends to take center stage. The opportunity for reflection may not emerge during the first semester, particularly in the wake of the more im- mediate, recurring pressures of grading and classroom management.

If the first semester for new teachers is just isolated chaos, what value does it possess for critical investigation? While the laboring qualities of composition instruction may be magnified in new teachers, I believe looking at new teachers opens up room for reflection about a broader split between theory and practice. Ultimately, we need to understand what of what we do is essential and consider the extent to which how we practice has something to do with how we learn to think about writing instruction, and, of course, vice versa. I invoke here Lisa Ede's call for "thinking through practice," which "looks for productive ways to place the two in dialogue. It looks, as well, for ways to call attention to contradictions and paradoxes that are sometimes overlooked in scholarly work" (*Situating Composition* 121). The following accounts feature two teachers, Shirley and Tess, as they struggle to make sense of process pedagogy, grading, and classroom management. Each of these struggles exists in a middle place between theory and practice, between staying alive—laboring—and holding one's head above the water for any length of time. With a mind toward this "middle place," my discussion in this chapter shifts between storytelling, critical reflection on existing composition scholarship, and reading each in terms of Arendt's ideas about labor. Ultimately, thinking through and against Arendt asks that we resist dichotomies (what Ann E. Berthoff has referred to as "killer dichotomies"), privileging one aspect of the classroom over another (qtd. in Ede, *Situating Composition* 103). In resisting these overly simplified associations, I believe we can explore more fully the embedded, complex, and at times contradictory goals of effective theory and practice.

LABORING CLASSROOMS IN A POST-PROCESS FIELD: "I DON'T KNOW HOW TO TEACH WRITING!"

While the process movement has been critiqued broadly, elements of process-based instruction are standard in many first-year writing courses and also mark many new teachers' first sense of "what to do" in the classroom.[2] At Public U, new graduate student teachers are required to take the teaching practicum during their first semester, which is designed to introduce them to issues of composition pedagogy and theory. However, these introductions are often fraught with graduate students' anxiety about existing teaching situations, since they take the practicum while teaching their first writing course. This creates a strained relationship between theory and practice, between ideas and experience. They are following a syllabus they did not design and trying to survive in the classroom while reading snapshots of theory. Therefore, graduate students tend to fit a cursory knowledge of process theory, rather uncomfortably, into the practical, everyday needs of their first classrooms. They have little room for thinking critically about existing scholarship and little time and space for thoughtful, pedagogical decision making. When new teachers express frustration at reading theory in the practicum, they are really expressing their desire for survival tools for day-to-day classroom existence. However, this frustration is generally misdirected at the theoretical readings on the practicum syllabus. In an attempt to apply pedagogical tools, writing process strategies can function much like Arendtian laboring, where drafting, grading, and revision activities are repeated almost mechanistically throughout the semester as a way of keeping the course functioning while the broader goals of the process movement are overlooked and any opportunity for exploration or reconsideration of these goals are closed off.

Tess and Shirley both struggled with their acquisition of strategies for teaching writing. Tess, in particular, was most expressive with her struggle around process-oriented instruction. She felt this tension very early in the semester; I received an email from her that stands as one of the most poignant of the entire study. With a truly desperate tone, Tess wrote the following:

> I'm freaking out! Today I collected 44 papers (first drafts that I am not grading, but will mark up for revision), and I don't really have any idea what to do with them. I have written "A" papers all my life, but I don't know how to look at other people's work. And, all of the papers I have written (including at the college level) were exactly the 5-paragraph format, which we aren't really supposed to drill into students. [I've been told to] focus on the argument, but I am not sure what that means. Am I looking for the opinion (agree/disagree) they have formed

about the texts? Argument as opposed to summary? I don't know how to verbalize the technical aspect of writing. Also, we have all these weeks set aside for "paper discussion" [on the syllabus]. I don't know what that means either. I DON'T KNOW HOW TO TEACH WRITING!!! How should I be setting up these classes? What do the students need to understand from these paper discussions? I am so worried right now that I am doing everything wrong, and that by mid-semester my class still won't make sense of how this comp class is structured and how it will help them. (15 Sept.)

There are many factors at work in this email. Among them is a tone of real urgency and desperation. Tess identified a shortcoming in her ability to communicate and share writing skills that she herself already possessed: "I have written 'A' papers all my life, but I don't know how to look at other people's work." Further, she had acquired new information—the five-paragraph format she's used successfully in the past is not encouraged—that seemed to rob her of any confidence in her existing knowledge. While Tess referred to her own inability to "verbalize the technical aspect of writing," beneath the surface of this admission was an urgency that undermined any desire to understand content, form, or theory. Tess needed to know what to say to students. Faced with the risk of having nothing to tell them about how to write, the legitimacy of her teaching was at stake.

While Tess's concern about how to teach writing signified a deeper need for theoretical understanding, her current situation did not allow it. This became increasingly clear when, toward the end of the correspondence, her focus shifted to her students and what they needed. She questioned what students "need to understand" about the paper discussions and expressed her concern that by mid-semester, her students "still won't make sense of how this comp class is structured and how it will help them." Here Tess found herself in a position to convince students of the course's inherent value, but she was unsure of how to do this and understandably was herself unclear about the academic benefits of the course content. In a later email, she became more desperate in her efforts to "sell" students on the course: "I told them they could revise as much as they want and I'd sit down with them as much as they want—and I could add the addendum that I could tell them if their papers are passing or not" (20 Sept.). It is here that process strategies emerge as "what to do" in the writing course. Traces of process-oriented writing instruction, written into the syllabus, functioned here for Tess from a purely laboring standpoint. Her efforts were based upon the necessity of "saving" the course: "my class still won't make sense of how this comp class is structured and how it will help them."

Tess's "paper discussion" days that were written into the syllabus were meant to be dedicated to peer review and revision. Perhaps one or two students' papers could have been used as examples for the entire class to work on while the teacher modeled critical feedback and revision strategies. Tess did not instinctively know this, which was understandable for someone who had never taught or studied composition. Paper discussion time is, undoubtedly, dedicated largely to process-oriented strategies for teaching writing. This was Tess's first attempt at process instruction in the classroom; her reading of some foundational process work—like that of Linda Flower and John R. Hayes—seemed unlikely to calm her fears. Instead, she needed to understand process strategies from the standpoint of "what to do" with this class, how to not only get through the next day but also convince students (and herself) that this was a real, legitimate course and that she was legitimately at its helm. The inevitable by-product of this situation is that writing process strategies are positioned—for the new teacher and for students—overwhelmingly as laboring activities, exclusively as "process-as-practice," the "stuff" to do to make the class really happen. When I use this term, "process-as-practice," I am not attempting to brand "practice" with a negative label. Instead, I mean to suggest a kind of problematic exclusiveness, where process pedagogy has been dislocated from the various debates, rationales, and theories that galvanized its earlier popularity.

Ultimately, this initial relationship with writing process is problematic for many reasons, many of which reflect existing critiques of the process movement. Most notably, it forges a relationship between students and teacher that ignores the real value and depth of students' development on which process theory is founded. Process-as-practice undermines a new teacher's potential to be a student of writing development, in much the same way that an overly formulaic approach to process instruction can fit diverse student needs into a limiting, generic set of predetermined practices. Instead, the nuts and bolts of process-as-practice function as tools for surviving, getting from the beginning of the class to the end. Paper discussion days threaten to operate as a kind of thoughtless process in the new teacher's classroom. Reflecting on the much-needed scrutiny of the process movement, Ede points out the dangers of distilling process instruction to "the potentially mechanistic, and even industrial, connotations of this term" ("Reading" 35). Ede goes on to explain, "To the extent that this mechanistic conception of process has literally and metaphorically informed both the teaching of and research on writing, it has inevitably oversimplified and distorted a phenomenon whose richness and complexity we have yet to adequately acknowledge" (35).

When Tess and her peers did get the chance to read some process theory, they were at risk of digesting it as more of a nuisance than as something that could deepen their intellectual engagement with what they were doing in the classroom. Because process-as-practice feeds so understandably into "what to do each day," theory follows either as something to overlook or as stripped for its immediate applicability alone. New teachers can receive the two as mutually exclusive rather than as designed to enhance and deepen the other. Ede explains in *Situating Composition* the dangers of narrow and hierarchical categories for practice and theory, where "practice participates in the social construction of reality" (120). It is in such a context that we have teachers who practice and scholars who theorize, rather than a confluence of labels and approaches to knowledge making.

Early formation of these categories can be at work in graduate students' first initiation into their own pedagogical development. I received an email from Shirley in which she reflected on the practicum, lamented the fact that she had to lose a creative writing elective to it, and imagined a more useful course. Along the way, she revealed a very telling understanding of the practicum's purpose and the value of training writing teachers:

I basically accept the practicum as a necessary evil. Certainly, some of the reading inspired ideas on how to teach, and I've been working on practical implementation of those ideas, but I still feel the practicum would have been more useful if it started in late July or early August, and I'm still not happy about losing an elective to it. I do appreciate the effort he [the practicum professor] has made to make it more practical. The tip sheets he's sent out, and his suggestions on ways to teach other authors were very helpful, more so, I think, than reading theory. I wonder how he feels about teaching a service course. (5 Oct.)

Here, Shirley's thought "I wonder how he feels about teaching a service course" clarified her understanding of the practicum's work of preparing her as a writing teacher and, subsequently, the nature of her tasks in the classroom. Essentially, from Shirley's perspective, the strings were cut: teaching the practicum was not about introducing new graduate students to composition theory and rhetorical analysis. Rather, it was about participating in their struggle to survive. The professor teaching the practicum was assessed in terms of his immediate value only, "the effort he has made to make it more practical." Because this faculty member had successfully "made it more practical," he was suddenly "teaching a service course." This connotation, of course, devalued the practicum syllabus and its potential for scholarly engagement or intellectual challenge. The practicum, then, had also become about surviving, about helping the new teachers to do things in their classrooms that would get them from Point A to Point B. They needed to get through the semester, to implement strategies—a series of drafting and revising sessions, for example—and either assistance in doing so or, at least, less theory. In this context, the training of new teachers is yet another arm of the laboring wheel.

LEARNING AND DOING: LABOR AND THE THEORY/PRACTICE DIVIDE

The prospect of what to teach each day or, more specifically, how to teach writing is at the foundation of labor in the writing classroom.

The question of "how" for the laboring new graduate student teacher demands practical, applicable answers, often at the expense of questions about how the field has theorized or critiqued a particular approach. Interestingly, for our field's rich, though short, history with the study of writing process, I would argue that the preparation of new writing teachers in this context is still under-theorized.[3] We can argue that new teachers learn by doing, and this would be a valid argument; however, from the vantage point of the new writing teacher, the challenge of what to do each day looms. The students whose writing is most in need of repair pose an added challenge: How does a new teacher get such students' writing from failing to passing, particularly if the new teacher feels he or she does not "know how to verbalize the technical aspect of writing"? Questions like this one can function as a driving force behind graduate student teachers' pedagogical approach.

At Public U, the required teaching practicum course provides graduate students with an introductory knowledge of composition theory. While valuable in its own right, such a knowledge base is not necessarily instructive in terms of what to do with a struggling student's paper, at least not from the urgent perspective of the drowning new teacher. The syllabus, under the subtitle "How Do We Teach Revision?," required graduate students to read Sondra Perl and Nancy Sommers. While the contribution of Perl, for example, to process theory can not be discounted, study of her work serves more as an introduction to innovations in writing research than as a pedagogical resource for the new graduate student struggling to survive in the classroom. Because new graduate students at Public U must teach during their first semester, most inevitably teach writing for the first time without a method for doing so. In many cases, graduate students are former undergraduates who simply got good grades on papers. With this fact their only connection to writing instruction, many are at a loss with students who struggle far more than they ever did.

The use of uniform syllabi and assignments are insufficient handholding when it comes to really having something (or some way) to teach. For Public U's new graduate student teachers, a set syllabus is distributed during orientation that includes paper assignments they can use and, of course, preselected readings. Thus, all new teachers enrolled in the teaching practicum course teach the same syllabus. At the same time, they are also encouraged to make changes as they see fit. However, many feel sufficiently uncomfortable with their new task, so much so that rewriting assignments or substituting course readings feels like only more pressure. Instead, they venture forth. At some point in the semester, they may find themselves trying to explain or justify a paper assignment they did not come up with and may not fully understand. Worse, grading is an additional challenge when one lacks a clear vision for the assignment. Out of this foreign course blueprint, new writing teachers learn some kind of method for teaching writing. They formulate something because they must: students are submitting work; many are failing; most are struggling and asking for assistance. How should a new instructor handle a barrage of questions regarding the new paper assignment (What are you looking for here? How can I get an A? How do I write a good introduction?)? Despite the presence of teaching mentors, advanced graduate students with significant teaching experience, many new graduate student teachers are amply overwhelmed by such questions. While mentors can help new teachers navigate early challenges, participants in my study often viewed them—perhaps erroneously—as authoritative "police" or as too burdened with their own graduate work to provide real support.[4]

Tess's and Shirley's expectations and questions around how to teach and what to teach reveal somewhat contradictory pressure and support. The predetermined materials graduate students have in hand for their first teaching experiences do little to satiate the pressure to know how to instruct students in writing; at the same time, these materials push new teachers through the semester, at least as filler. Expectations that new teachers will enact our field's accepted process-oriented approaches to writing instruction parallel the set syllabus for new teachers. Neither Tess nor Shirley was invested in a particular approach, nor had either made intellectual commitments to theorized models. In her contribution to *In Our Own Voice*, Stacia Dunn Neeley writes:

I realized that I was alone, but not independent: the process approach by which I was expected to guide students through a "cognitive spiral" from personal, "egocentric writing" to a socially aware "ecocentric writing," the six modes I was expected to employ to fulfill this spiraling, the suggested syllabus, and the two texts I was expected to justify to my students were all of someone else's choosing. My students would supposedly "spiral upward" toward those more advanced writing tasks that the university would demand. While trying to find ways to make them spiral, I was experiencing full-fledged vertigo. . . . I was twenty-three years old, nervous, malleable, and conditioned to conventional classroom reality. (20)

Neeley's concerns show a lumping of process theory with all the other ambiguous, overwhelming responsibilities new teachers must navigate, like predetermined syllabi and course readings. New teachers are not in a position, typically, to assess the value of process theory or chart the development of composition as a field. Rather, they are in a sea of suggested and/or required practices that they must immediately make their own. For these reasons, I am not attempting to critique process theory per se but to consider it as yet another part of new teachers' sink-or-swim laboring experience in the first semester.

The significance of learning process theory in the context Neeley describes resonates with long-standing critiques of the process movement. As Joseph Harris writes in his 1997 work, *A Teaching Subject*, "My concerns . . . are not aimed against the proposition that writing is a process—which, again, strikes me as a claim that is true, banal, and of a real, if limited, use—but against a view of teaching that places some vision of the composing process (rather than an interest in the work of students) at the center of a course in writing" (57). For Tess and Shirley, who were following process approaches in the same way they were following a set syllabus, this loss was doubled: they were not studying writers' development but following set practices. In the midst of this rule following, the effects can be dramatic. In her contribution to Lad Tobin and Thomas Newkirk's collection *Taking Stock*, Ede writes of this danger:

But any consideration of the role that the writing process movement has played in effecting institutional change must also acknowledge the ease with which these changes not only can be
but at times have been co-opted and commodified—by textbooks that oversimplified and rigidified a complex phenomenon,
by overzealous language arts coordinators and writing program
administrators who assumed that the process approach to teaching could be "taught" in one or two in-service sessions, by all
those (myself included) who forgot that the very term "writing
process movement" refers not to a concrete and material reality
but to an ideologically-charged construct. ("Reading" 35)

If we combine the legitimacy of Harris's concerns with the fact that
process-oriented teaching practices may be built into new teachers'
requirements in the way Ede describes, we have reason to reevaluate
how we introduce new teachers to process theory and to assess what
it is we think process theory can teach new teachers.

Process pedagogy can function as yet another predetermined
assignment for new teachers and thus stands to take on the shape
of the thoughtless, everyday responsibilities necessary to survival
rather than a theoretically engaged choice. For Arendt, laboring is
quintessentially thoughtless—"where one must eat in order to labor
and must labor in order to eat"—and thus, I argue, an insufficient
approach to teaching, which surely requires intellectual commitments and strategies (*Human Condition* 87). Harris reminds readers
of Don Murray's famous call for "'teaching writing as process not
product,'" a phrase, he writes, that "was quickly to gain the status
(and perhaps meaninglessness) of a mantra" (*Teaching Subject* 56).
While the conversation in the field may have moved on, process
pedagogies remain a component of most first-year writing classrooms
and marked, significantly, the early practice of the graduate students
I studied. Ede affirms, "Despite widespread agreement on the part
of scholars that composition is in important ways post-process, engagement with process still manifests itself in both our classrooms
and in the textbooks that can play such a critical role in teaching"
(*Situating Composition* 98).

To complicate things further, we must revisit Harris's critique that the fascination with the writing process itself detracts from the focus on students' actual work. The concerns of Harris and others about excessive focus on the process itself reveal an interesting departure from founding tenets of the process movement. Peter Elbow's early articulation of these tenets celebrates personal responsibility and individualism: "Many people are now trying to become less helpless, both personally and politically: trying to claim more control over their own lives. One of the ways people most lack control over their own lives is through lacking control over their words" (qtd. in Ede, *Situating Composition* 96). However, this struggle for control through the writing process is quickly overshadowed by "the extent to which both its methods and its conclusions depended upon the reduction of students, in all their diversity, into a construct called the student writer, and of writing, with its rich multiplicity, into student writing" (Ede, "Reading" 35).

Arendt's ideas about labor uncover complicated tensions in our evolving "talk" about process. Arendt argues that, with the advent of scientific discovery, scientists' focus became increasingly on the process of making rather than on the product outcome. Accordingly, production itself began to mirror the biological process of laboring: "It was as though the means, the production process or development, was more important than the end, the finished product. The reason for this shift is obvious: the scientist made only in order to know, not in order to produce things, and the product was a mere by-product, a side effect" (*Human Condition* 297). Here, only the process itself is a source of study and value while the product is largely overlooked. In their foundational piece "A Cognitive Process Theory of Writing," Flower and Hayes embody Arendt's worries in their argument for cognitive process work: "The problem with stage descriptions of writing is that they model the growth of the written product, not the inner process of the person producing it" (367). A critical response follows in Harris's concern that student work is ignored for the sake of studying the process itself and in Ede's charge about the process movement's generic "student writer." In his critique of Janet Emig, Harris notes her sharp distinction between reflexive and extensive writing: "The writing researcher (working exclusively in the extensive mode) makes knowledge about the composing process available for teachers to use in encouraging students to write more expressively or reflexively. Science enables art" (*Teaching Subject* 59). Harris goes on to question the seamlessness of such a relationship and charges that the product itself is lost in our fixation on process.

Ultimately, there are three major players involved in the dynamics between process writing and Arendtian labor: the student writer; scholarly critics of process pedagogy; and writing teachers. Of course, there can be a conflation of roles between the scholar and the writing teacher; however, the nature of first-year writing in the university necessitates far more teachers in classrooms who are not also theorizing, studying, and publishing their work on writing pedagogy. This three-part relationship is in no way simple. While Tess "must eat in order to labor and must labor in order to eat" in her application of process-as-practice in her first writing classroom, surely we do practice an injustice to suggest it is devoid of thought or to position it as a kind of hierarchical bottom in the types of work we do with student writing. In fact, process theorists' attention to the writing process itself can be read as an attempt to value what lies beneath these more mechanical functions, evidenced by Flower and Hayes's pointing to the "inner process of the person producing it." Yet, these efforts come full circle in later, post-process charges—like those of Harris and Ede—that suggest the study of the process obscures an idea of "who" this "person producing it" really is. We end up, inevitably, at Arendt's worry that scientists "made only in order to know, not in order to produce things."

While some feminists have critiqued Arendt's concept of labor for "ghettoizing" biological processes to the (typically feminine) domestic sphere, others have argued that this is merely a misreading of Arendt, who resists gendering what she sees as broader, more interrelated human capacities.[5] Arendt does equate laboring with biology, with a kind of essential pull that isolates the laborer from other spheres of activity, like work or action. But if Arendt's categories are merely meant to represent potential capacities, not to label us immovably as "what" we are, something is deeply wrong when we only labor, when we tend exclusively to one capacity. Critiques of the process movement, then, at once come to underscore the "problem" of endless labor—or the consequences of a hyper-focus on process—while also highlighting an ongoing, problematic gap in who labors and who does not, who makes and who runs endlessly, who thinks and who does not have time to think. Ultimately, while many scholars may agree that the field has long been post-process for all—and more—of the reasons Harris and Ede underscore, these critiques do not fix the problem of labor, the problem represented in Tess's and Shirley's conception of "process-as-practice," as an immediate but also fleeting solution to making the writing class real. The enduring question becomes, then: What is the long-term, disciplinary effect of this gap between well-grounded critique and the realities of how new writing teachers may learn to teach writing? My work here falls short of answering this question. Instead, I believe these stories of Tess's and Shirley's initial adaptation of process pedagogy, particularly when read through Arendt, become a model for thinking about the consequences of dangerous laboring, for recognizing such laboring when it occurs, and for rethinking such scenarios to ultimately disrupt them.

AUTHORITY AND CONTROL: THE LABORING WHEELS OF GRADING AND CLASSROOM MANAGEMENT

For the new graduate student teachers in my study, pedagogical approach was not the only facet of their teaching that was susceptible to the difficulties of Arendtian laboring. Their navigation of students' rebellions, questions, and frustrations was also easily swept up into a kind of cyclical, repetitive process that often left them breathless. In the following classroom accounts, I describe Tess's and Shirley's struggles with classroom management—the maintenance of a healthy, positive classroom atmosphere—and grading.

Classroom management and the grading burden entangled in Shirley's first-semester struggle with "the 8:40" class. Aside from its challenge to wakefulness, the class became a kind of communication deadlock. Students seemed to resent Shirley and the class itself; Shirley resented them for their reticence and apparent negativity.

With both sides of the classroom in a huff, classroom management felt like wading through quicksand. Shirley and I exchanged many conversations about her dreaded "8:40," one in which she described the situation as follows:

> I'm having a minor freak out about teaching. My 8:40 class is a wall of passive resistance. I tried a role-playing exercise with them, thinking that if nothing else, it would get them all to participate, and they hated it. At this point, I'm beginning to feel that their hatred of the syllabus is extending to me, because I'm getting some downright evil looks in my direction. (email, 11 Oct.)

At this point in the semester, students were frustrated with the assigned syllabus. The readings for the course included Raymond Williams, Chinua Achebe, and Antonio Gramsci. Gramsci was received with confusion and frustration in most of the new TAs' classrooms, and Shirley's group was no exception. She struggled to make the reading more accessible while she herself searched for ways to both understand and explain Gramsci. In the meantime, student resentment was high and naturally directed toward instructors, despite the fact that they had not selected such readings. While students' reticence in the classroom may have been a product of their own sense of being "doomed" by readings they felt they could not understand, Shirley assumed responsibility for their dissatisfaction.

Tensions around the "wall" continued to build. Finally, I received an email from Shirley that declared, "Today would have to be the worst class of the semester." Most of her students failed to read the Mary Louise Pratt essay, "Arts of the Contact Zone," for class, leaving her without a real approach or lesson for the day. Her response was to utilize credit toward final grades and distribute punishments and rewards accordingly. She wrote:

> Five out of the seventeen of them actually read the Pratt and showed up in class to discuss it. They were surprised that there was a reading assignment, never mind that it's in the syllabus and posted on the Blackboard [course website] announcements. I made them read it in class and write out summaries,

and they were resentful, but so was I. I'm giving the people who read it extra credit for the day, and the people who didn't are failing class participation for the day. Now I just have to let it go and begin the discussion on Thursday as if today didn't happen. Thank god it's the last reading for the semester. (7 Nov.)

In this context, classroom management hinged upon getting students to do their work for the day. Students' failure (or refusal) to be prepared for class effectively prevented Shirley's lesson from happening; her response was to use grading to punish and reward. Shirley assumed that students' motivation here was connected to grades. She believed that the prospect of a lower grade would sufficiently inspire students to be responsible for their reading assignments.

While Shirley contended with students' "wall of passive resistance" and subsequent dissatisfaction with the course, Tess found herself dealing with powerful—and publicly vocal—resistance in the form of a particularly expressive student. By 1 October of the first semester, Tess had identified her problem student and dubbed him "Philosophy Phil." While tensions between Tess and Phil would escalate to problematic proportions later in the semester (and will be dealt with more extensively in chapter 3), at this early stage, Tess merely struggled over how to handle Phil in the classroom forum. In the classroom, Phil was the student who consistently posed public challenges and tried to catch the teacher off guard. He wanted to show Tess up or prove her wrong. He also had a knack for over-analysis and pushing an issue to its combustible limits, hence Tess's nickname for him, "Philosophy Phil." From the vantage point of a new teacher, Phil's public antics threatened her authority and the viability of the class at its core. Perhaps a more experienced teacher would have seen through Phil's "testing" and would also have recognized more quickly that other students could see through him, too. However, for Tess, Phil's classroom presence was a consistent and deadly threat to her validity as the teacher, the fact of her subject knowledge, and other students' acceptance of her authority.

I received an email from Tess recounting a situation where Phil questioned her and she floundered. Specifically, Phil asked, "What's a verb?" and Tess stumbled over the right words in response. In the email message below, she was angry with herself for not having a more effective response to a seemingly simple question, and she lamented the danger of saying "I don't know" to students' inquiries:

> Why can't I do that in the classroom? I know that we are supposed to be comfortable with saying "I don't know" and redirecting the question, but how are we supposed to be comfortable doing that? Because of my inexperience, I already lack confidence; if I say I don't know, then I might as well sit down and let the students run the class. I feel like I have to know the answer, or my students won't respect me; they'll lose faith in me and this class. (1 Oct.)

Here, Tess perceived the consequences of "I don't know" to be crushing. Simply put, she thought that the teacher could not remain "the teacher" if he or she did not know an answer to a student's question. In fact, as Tess pointed out, to "not know" means that one basically has the same authority, or knowledge base, as any of the students in the class. Accordingly, she maintained, "I might as well sit down and let the students run the class." Tess's approach to classroom management and her own authority had a "do or die" quality, one that clearly established a hierarchical relationship between the teacher-as-knowledge-source and students as recipients of this knowledge, much like Paulo Freire's well-known "banking concept" discussed in *Pedagogy of the Oppressed*. Her appearance before the class was almost strictly about survival, at least according to the rhetoric of this particular situation. When she failed, even once, she believed that she lost her students' loyalty to her as a teacher and to the class as a whole.

Toward the end of her email, Tess took a slightly more positive focus, though she lamented her current "growing pains." Regardless, the correspondence ended with her admittance of an overemphasis on Philosophy Phil in her teaching and her jokingly wishful thinking that this job could be easier:

> Sometimes, I have Philosophy Phil in mind when I do my lesson plans, because I don't want to have any loopholes where he can catch me off guard. It's obsessive and unhealthy, I know;

and, there probably should be loopholes for the sake of class discussion. If this happened last week, I would be having a breakdown—I suck, my students see right through me, they hate me, I'm wasting their time! But, today, it's different. I realize that with time, I will improve my technique for redirecting questions—right now, though, the growing pains are really uncomfortable and discouraging. I just wish there was a tip-sheet for responding to questions that take me by surprise: Techniques for Redirecting Questions in Every Possible Situation. Is that asking too much? (1 Oct.)

Tess's focus on the particularly difficult student in her class surely fed into her survival/do-or-die approach to classroom management. She planned her lessons defensively, as if preparing for an imminent attack. It's unfortunate that, in her very first semester, she was confronted with a student who presented so much extra stress. However, Tess's attitude about students' loyalty and respect, as they related to her perception of her own authority, seemed to exist also separately from "Phil." While Phil was a catalyst, Tess perceived all the students as potentially or easily convinced of her lack of knowledge or authority. Certainly, Phil did not make this insecurity any lighter or easier to manage. However, this quest for authority seemed to be a pervasive struggle as Tess adjusted to teaching. Efforts to gain this authority seemed, in her eyes, to be fleeting, weak, and constantly in need of reassertion. Any public disruption to her status threatened to wipe away any authority students had granted her.

Tess's worries about the complete loss of authority were not unfounded, nor were her struggles in the classroom confined to Phil. One evening in October, I received a phone call from an overwhelmed Tess. A graduate of Public U, Tess was familiar with the composition course from the student side. However, when she gave out a bunch of Ds and Fs as a teacher, she never thought students would revolt. The low grades had two major sources of inspiration, according to Tess: first, "they [the students] thought if they fixed the individual comments they should get a passing grade," and second, the supervising mentor advised to grade tough. Tess asserted in a follow-up email, "I respect her opinion because she's speaking from a position of authority—and I bought into that—and I've seen other professors do stuff like this and it kind of worked because they (the students) got much more invested in the class—they had to think, 'I can't blow this off'" (7 Oct.).

Despite Tess's rationale for the tough grades and regardless of whether or not they deserved them, the students were in full riot mode. Tess shared with me that, during class, a couple of them "were on their feet, arguing and pointing at me." She felt that they were organizing before her eyes while she was left to defend a program and course she didn't even completely understand. At once impressed by how much they cared and simultaneously pressured by her own role, she described the scene: "They were all concerned and interested in the comp course. It was so political—even with the portfolio—they were uniting. They were so critical and skeptical of the course and the inconsistencies in the program. So it was also critical of me—they asked, 'How is your system beneficial to us? Why are you right?'" (email, 20 Sept.). Here, Tess was actually moved by students' resistance, their investment in their grades and interest in the course itself. She explained that students "didn't have confidence that they'd improve, that writing is a process and they'll improve." Tess was unsure of how to move the process along, too, asking me, "I think I write about the same on each draft—should I comment more on their first draft?" It seemed as if all the pressure was on her to show students their improvement; grades functioned here as the hard evidence for students that there was hope and as an authority bargaining chip for the new teacher. With her sense of authority tied so tightly to her role as grader, Tess felt particularly vulnerable when confronted with students' challenges to the course rules and the grades they received. In a sense, the viability of Tess's role was undermined: rather than validate her choices, students called them and the course itself into question.

Although she quickly tried to appease students with a "tip sheet," a checklist for their writing, soon the appeasement would take on more desperate proportions. When students showed no signs of understanding or acceptance, Tess got more desperate for compliance, as quoted previously: "I told them they could revise as much as they want and I'd sit down with them as much as they want—and I could add the addendum that I could tell them if their papers are passing or not." Authority was quickly turned on its head, and grading functioned as a kind of trap or prison. Not only were students demanding certain grades, but Tess found herself working harder for students so that they could have those grades. The authority associated with grading required constant maintenance.

By the end of our conversation, Tess admitted to her exhaustion, although she took on her added responsibilities with graceful acceptance. She shared her preoccupation with the "revolt" experience: "I'm trying to write this Theory paper [for an introductory graduate course] and was sick all day long—because the 9:40 class just kept popping up in my mind" (email, 7 Oct.). Yet again, she was resigned to her added responsibilities because she chose to view the experience as instructive for her, perhaps a facet of her own education as a teacher. She also seemed to interpret the students as very "right" about their frustration with the low grades and justified in their confusion about the course itself (such as why portfolios were graded pass/fail by a committee rather than by Tess herself). As she explained to me, "I saw this as a mid-semester evaluation. I'm willing to adjust. At first I took it all to heart. But now, I'm trying to use this constructively—to say to them, 'I heard you. This is my response.' This is their class—they have just as much responsibility as I do in how the class is run" (email, 7 Oct.). Of course, as students gained in authority regarding how the class was run, it seemed Tess had to double her workload. Furthermore, some sources of student frustration, like the portfolio review, were never Tess's choice. Thus, her language of responsibility, "This is my response," seemed to assume fully a largely misdirected critique. We are left with these important questions: What kind of impact does this introduction to grades and authority have on the new writing teacher? How does this experience shape his or her formulation of good writing and good teaching?

GRADES AND CLASSROOM MANAGEMENT AS
ARENDTIAN LABOR: THE COSTS OF SURVIVAL

Arendt describes the nature of labor: "The process [life process] can continue only provided that no worldly durability and stability is permitted to interfere, only as long as all worldly things, all end products of the production process, are fed back into it at an ever-increasing speed" (*Human Condition* 256). In other words, laboring is inclined only toward endlessness and impermanence, as is the biological system after which it is modeled. Its opposite, work or fabrication, implies the creation of something lasting; that which is "lasting" is not aligned with the life process, for Arendt, as the life process only proceeds into decay and, thus, the ongoing biological process itself. These categories never function as neatly separate; as humans, we constantly possess the potential to engage in each aspect of the human condition. While it is important to explore how these aspects of Arendt's theoretical model overlap and blur with others as new teachers experiment and struggle, I am also interested in considering what happens when we explore some facet of new teaching in a more isolated way. That is, what do grading and classroom management look like as labor? What features of these classroom tasks are fed endlessly into a kind of cyclical process? How does this kind of pedagogical laboring shape a new teacher's perception of what it means to teach writing? How does it shape his or her understanding of the field of composition studies? And where might there be potential for new teachers to see tangible products or lasting rewards for their efforts, for labor to become something more enduring?

Cyclical, dangerously consumptive grading is linked closely to issues of "classroom management"—a term I use hesitantly, as this idea of "management" suggests a particularly authoritative classroom—and thinking through and beyond Arendt on such issues uncovers essential considerations. When we apply Arendt to these concepts, we are challenged to think about laboring in two somewhat opposing directions. On the one hand, we can understand labor much as Arendt wishes us to: we must feed into the system endlessly, as our efforts are sufficient only for mere sustenance and thus immediately lost. However, alternately, we might think more centrally about new graduate students behaving as laborers while simultaneously generating some tangible rewards that only others—those outside their immediate experience, such as university administrators and even students—can see and reap. Tess's allowance of endless revisions and conferences and her toying with the idea that she could tell students in conferences if their papers were passing or not were merely sufficient, from her vantage point, for preventing yet another rebellion or total "shut down" of the flow of the course. She was running in a grading wheel: interest in what these papers looked like was not mentioned, nor did she note how the writing of individual students might evolve conceptually, structurally, or linguistically over the course of multiple grading, conferencing, and revising sessions.

But students did, in fact, take a kind of tangible reward away from Tess's labor that she did not seem to register: abundant feedback, opportunities for multiple revisions, and even multiple grades. Tess did not seem to accumulate these benefits, as she was endlessly dedicated to helping students to get the grades they wanted so that they did not overturn her classroom again. Arendt's discussion of labor—mirroring Tess's experience—leaves out the possible, longstanding gains of those who feed off of the laborer's efforts. Grading thus functions as an attempt by new teachers to stay alive in the classroom; they perceive that their authority is aligned solely with the fact that they have the power to give students the grades they want. However, the authority is vested in the grades themselves. New teachers have become more of a factory for such grades than facilitators of writing development, at least in their perspective. In this sense, new teachers' experience is clearly split between grading as a means of quantifying students' development and grading as a means of maintaining a "managed" classroom. As a new teacher operates in this split, a number of important questions arise about the teacher's pedagogical growth. What does the teacher learn about writing assessment? About the relationship between grades and revision? About the goals of conferencing and feedback? About the classroom community, including expectations for student engagement, participation, and the teacher/student relationship?

While a new graduate student teacher negotiates his or her authority and pedagogical approach, student resistance and frustration can be a steady presence in the first-year writing classroom. As we well know, many undergraduate students come to first-year composition insecure about their own writing abilities, confused (or doubtful) about the role of writing in their professional (and even personal) lives, and often grumbling about the requirement status of the course. After all, it's a course most students are required to take and at which few really excel. Successful composition instructors need some strategy for classroom management, given the environmental potential; new graduate student teachers usually have to shape theirs via trial and error. I am reminded of David Bartholomae's "Quentin," in his classic essay "The Tidy House: Basic Writing in the American Curriculum," who so powerfully embodies the kind of student resistance that leaves a new teacher dumbfounded. Bartholomae describes Quentin's written response to his admittedly obscure assignment, which I will quote at length here:

> Then there is a string of scratched out sentences, and then the words "stop" and "lose" written in caps. Then there is this:
>
>> Let go back and survive, to survive it is necessary to kill or be kill, this what existentialism is all about.
>> Man will not survive, he is a asshole.
>> STOP
>> The story in the books or meanless stories and I will not elaborate on them This paper is meanless, just like the book, But, I know the paper will not make it.
>> STOP.
>
> Then there are crossed out sentences. And the end, in what now looks like a page from *Leaves of Grass* or *Howl*, there is this:
>
>> I don't care.
>> I don't care.
>> about man and good and evil I don't care about this shit fuck this shit, trash and should be put in the trash can with this shit
>> Thank you very much
>> I lose again. (6)

Bartholomae goes on to consider the significance of this resistance in terms of students' grappling with the institutional and linguistic authority of the university. However, this passage is most valuable on two levels for purposes of this study. First, this kind of resistance is common (though not always as forcefully articulated) in student writing, class participation, demeanor, teacher evaluations, and so on. It also stands independent of, but tied to, the need of new teachers to carve out their own authority, legitimacy, and working relationships with students. In new teachers especially, authority and legitimacy have to be affirmed consistently; one "good class" is never enough.

Bartholomae's well-known Quentin story is valuable because of the interesting rhetorical parallels it runs to the Arendtian model of surviving, or necessity, and the precarious position of new teachers before a class for the first time. Quentin applies a kind of "do or die" analysis, not only in his definition of existentialism or the course reading but toward the future of his paper. He writes, "This paper is meanless, just like the book, But, I know the paper will not make it. STOP." Here, the student parallels his own writing with that of something that has "agreed upon" authority: his paper is meaningless, "just like the book." However, in his case, the paper will not make it, whereas the book obviously has, as evidenced by its publication status and by the fact that he has to write a paper on it. His use of the phrase "make it" implies a kind of life-or-death struggle and the possibility for transition into the kind of "permanence" Arendt associates with work, not labor. Laboring is only for Quentin's paper, not for the published author's book. Quentin's exhausted tone predicts that none of his papers will ever make it. Accordingly, he demonstrates a bitter resolve to an exclusive laboring experience as a writer, much like what we see in Shirley's and Tess's early experiences of teaching.

For new graduate student teachers like Shirley and Tess, effective classroom management is an essential component to survival and, yet, surviving itself comes with a kind of defeatism similar to Quentin's exhaustion about his cycle of failed writing attempts. Labor, for Arendt, does not stand still, and yet its efforts are consistently washed away. It echoes in Quentin's "I lose again," in Shirley's "Now I just have to let it go and begin the discussion on Thursday as if today didn't happen," and in Tess's "I feel like I have to know the answer, or my students won't respect me; they'll lose faith in me and this class." Looming above this struggle to survive is the constant threat of "death," evidenced by Tess's dismal prediction, "By mid-semester my class still won't make sense of how this comp class is structured and how it will help them." Tess, Shirley, and Quentin all perceived their experience in the composition class—writing assessment, instruction, and writing itself—exclusively as a laboring experience. They had no sense that their efforts would do more than get them to the next challenge and held no expectations for tangible or lasting reward. The desire to move their efforts from pure labor to something more lasting may have been at the root of both Quentin's anxieties and Tess's students' anxieties about the future of their writing and the status of their grades.

Interestingly, Tess and Bartholomae have more complicated relationships to their experiences as laborers. In Tess's case, we see a resignation to her laboring, an inability to see beyond the endlessness of her efforts. She did not rebel, like Quentin, but seemed to accept her inexperience as a teacher as a kind of guarantor of continued laboring. Bartholomae's reflection on his Quentin experience, too, points to the cyclical, "doomed" tendency of the basic writing curriculum to produce "basic writers"; however, Bartholomae also rejects his place in this system through an emphasis on a rigorous curriculum ("Tidy House" 18). Bartholomae writes about his early teaching experience many years beyond his own "first semester" and comes to it with much experience as a scholar and teacher of writing. It seems unlikely that many graduate students who have shared a similar first-semester experience will also share the specifics of Bartholomae's later career.

In part, new teachers' conflicts with labor—even if they are able to look back much later with new resolve—can be traced conceptually to "best practices" accounts in composition scholarship. In their 1997 attempt to improve the success of portfolio assessment, Susanmarie Harrington and Tere Molinder Hogue admit that their "no grades till semester's end" policy had students in a huff: "Over and over we read comments like, 'Why did I have to wait until after the semester was over to find out how I was doing?' 'I learned a lot from a great teacher but didn't like not getting any grades' . . . after reading such comments semester after semester, we realized that we needed to know more about why our students are so troubled" (55). Of course, theoretically speaking, Harrington and Molinder Hogue's withholding grades until portfolios had understandable rationale: "Responses to work always carry with them another chance to do it better. And portfolios thus get us out of some of the traps the studies I have mentioned identified: if we are not always grading, we are not always needing to justify grades" (57). Freedom from "always needing to justify grades" would bring much-desired relief for a new teacher like Tess; however, Tess's concerns about student participation and satisfaction with the course might have prevented her from implementing such a policy. Further, the authors attest, "the emphasis is, for the most part, on the process of the portfolio and not on the product of the portfolio. Portfolios enable us to be a coach during the semester, and a judge after the semester is over, and the literature focuses much more on coaching strategies than judging strategies" (57). While Tess clearly held fast to process as "the literature" instructs, she did so as a means of response to student concerns about "product," or grades. The balance she attempted to strike became, ultimately, no balance at all. What we ultimately see is a grading process that, unhinged from its end-product status, aligns with Arendt's ideas about the consequences of laboring, that "all worldly things, all end products of the production process, are fed back into it at an ever-increasing speed" (*Human Condition* 256). Some relief from grading pressure would perhaps allow the new writing teacher to develop a more refined eye for argument and other details of the writing process. However, as Tess demonstrated, the potential tangible gains for her instructional approach were subsumed in the "ever-increasing speed" with which she attempted to respond to negative student opinion.

In her well-known piece "On Not Being a Composition Slave," Maxine Hairston notes the dangerous cycle of endless grading and revisions, one that leaves many instructors "disillusioned with the students who do not seem to take their advice to heart. They suspect that too often students don't even read their comments, but look only at the grade" (119). Hairston acknowledges that graduate students, above all other composition teachers, are most susceptible to this kind of laboring: "They will either invest far more time than they can afford on student papers, or they will constantly feel guilty that they are not doing their job right" (119). Hairston's concern for the graduate student writing teacher rings of Tess's willingness to grade, comment, and conference "as much as they want," particularly in light of Tess's status as a first semester PhD student with demanding coursework.

The dangers of the ocean's undertow prove a useful metaphor for understanding the threat of Arendt's concept of laboring gone awry. For the strong, confident swimmer, undertow—a current that runs repeatedly from shore to sea—can be manageable and even escapable, but for the inexperienced and especially tired swimmer, the dangers can be disastrous. Much of Tess's and Shirley's experiences of being pulled with increasing depth into their already furious efforts parallel popular warnings about inexperienced swimmers' management of undertow and the ways in which their ever-more desperate efforts often lead only to further exhaustion. Instead, one basic online source advises endangered swimmers, "If a swimmer tires, he or she should tread water and float in the hopes that a rescuer arrives."[6] Arendt's insistence that labor is not a label for "who" or "what" we are but rather just a capacity for behavior frees her thinking from the categories she most despised, like thinking of the home as representative of "women's work," for example.[7] However, this metaphor of the drowning laborer and much-needed rescuer represents consequences that Arendt seems to escape problematically. Can what we do—like endless laboring—become who we are, professionally? If this danger exists—and I'd argue that it does—what are the consequences for new graduate students, just introduced to a field and to a writing classroom? Finally, who are the rescuers and how can they help?

Duane Roen, Lauren Yena, Veronica Pantoja, Eric Waggoner, and Susan K. Miller's edited collection, *Strategies for Teaching First-*

Year Composition, makes a concerted effort to rescue new teachers from the pull of endless laboring. In Lynn Langer Meeks, Joyce Kinkead, Keith VanBezooyan, and Erin Edwards's piece, "Fostering Classroom Civility," the authors describe teaching mentors' creation of a general contract for use by graduate student instructors to establish rules for classroom behavior. In surveying the instructors, the mentors found "no real consensus" among instructors on the contents of the document and were at first "hard-pressed to develop a document that would give some instructors something hard and fast to fall back on while accommodating those who wanted to run the classroom their own way" (205). Ultimately, the mentors settled on a contract, included in the college's required first-year writing handbook, which some instructors have students sign and others actually give quizzes on "to encourage them [the students] to read and review it" (206). The contract includes guidelines for instructor and student expectations, successful classroom behavior, and disciplinary consequences.

While "Fostering Classroom Civility" does not describe the long-term successes and failures of this behavioral contract, I think the effort around its creation speaks to the consequences of Arendtian laboring and also responds to these consequences at a point where Arendt's analysis falls short. While Arendt warns of a society committed exclusively to laboring, she fails to imagine the inevitable hierarchy of groups and individuals who somehow feed off laborers' efforts, nor does she think proactively about "rescuers" for the drowning laborer, or a still-relevant desire in the laborer to continue to survive or even to escape laboring. Mina Shaughnessy's words at the start of this chapter, which speak to the "drowning" student who finds "that it is both realistic and essential to work at surviving," do not fully represent Arendt's doomed laborer. Instead, in *The Human Condition* we hear in Arendt's worries about labor a kind of inevitability, a demise of the worst, most inescapable kind:

> The last stage of the laboring society . . . demands of its members a sheer automatic functioning, as though individual life had actually been submerged in the overall life process of the species and the only active decision still required of the

individual were to let go, so to speak, to abandon his still individually sensed pain and trouble of living, and acquiesce in a dazed, "tranquilized," functional type of behavior. (322)

Arendt's "tranquilized" laborer is not whom we hear in Tess, in Shirley, or even in Bartholomae's student, Quentin. Instead, each took on certain qualities or behaviors of Arendt's laborer while they also took clear action to express their outrage or to seek help out of their situations, even as they felt the inevitable pull toward further laboring. These examples add another layer to Arendtian labor and also make a call for action—for rescuers—and suggest that the consequences of labor may not be certain doom. Instead, the notion of rescuers seems to serve as a kind of buoy; we see this function in the efforts and hopes behind Meeks and her colleagues' student behavior contract and even in Quentin's idea that certain papers—like those of published authors—"make it." This is about doing more than laboring.

While we can—and will, in the next chapter—move to Arendt's concept of action as the stalwart against the ultimately ill-fated "laboring society," I believe Arendt makes this transition too seamlessly. The application of her ideas here requires further work and questioning than Arendt's theory alone allows. Indeed, Arendt's concepts give us fodder for Ede's "thinking through practice," for trying to imagine the effects, layers, and alternatives to graduate students' exclusive laboring as writing teachers. Accordingly, we are left with the following questions for further research: What are the exceptions or parasitic hierarchies around graduate students' laboring? In other words, while the graduate student may perceive that his or her efforts are subsumed by laboring, is this always the case? How can we recognize who benefits and determine what these benefits are? What happens to the laboring graduate student's long-term relationship to writing pedagogy and research? Are there aspects of writing instruction that must, in fact, function as labor, or do the most effective teachers strive for practice that continually exceeds the confines of labor alone? Where does our laboring arm leave our scholarly mind?

3

Teachers-as-Students: Work and Action in the Middle Space

> The redemption of life, which is sustained by labor, is worldliness, which is sustained by fabrication.
>
> —Hannah Arendt, *The Human Condition*

HANNAH ARENDT DEFINES ACTION as the moment in which we reveal ourselves in the public arena for others to see, hear, and remember as distinctive, memorable agents. In these moments we not only reveal who we are but also proclaim our love for the world because—when we "appear before others" in the spirit of "plurality"—we prevent its otherwise certain decay (Arendt, *Human Condition* 176). The life process is one that naturally runs into extinction, and it is only the human capacity for "interrupting it and beginning something new" that ultimately saves the world and reestablishes our connection to each other, our "worldliness" (246). Steeped in issues of public revelation and communal space, Arendtian action seems potentially fertile ground for thinking about new graduate students and their identification with classroom, university, and field. However, many relevant questions loom. First of all, who gets to be an actor, and why? Are we all eligible and capable at any moment, including the newest of teachers? What happens to action beyond its "moment"?

In order to better understand action, we must explore Arendt's ideas about action in relationship to a third human capacity: work. In the most preliminary sense, Arendt defines work as an activity that "fabricates the sheer unending variety of things whose sum constitutes the human artifice" (*Human Condition* 136). The objects we fabricate with our hands serve as monuments to the fact of our existence, evidence that we acted and spoke together. Artists, writers, storytellers, and builders, through the work of their hands, leave traces of events ("word and deed" as Arendt would say) that shape a history. We might think of work as an anchor in the whirlwind of nature—from which we come and into which we are eventually swept—that allows us to be connected over time rather than lost without a trace. Importantly, in workers' efforts to create monuments and the general "stuff" of the world, they also create a kind of arena, a space, in which action can happen at all and through which our self-defining words and deeds can be remembered. In a recent special issue of *Teachers College Record* dedicated to Arendt, editor Christopher Higgins aptly describes the relationship between work and action: "A world created by work alone would be like a stage set after the show has been closed" (420). Accordingly, in order to understand action as a kind of saving force against endless laboring, we must understand its dependency on work and vice versa. It is the collaboration and interconnected functioning of action and work that ultimately save the world, for Arendt.

Arendtian rhetoric that defines action as invention and beginning has reappeared in various approaches to pedagogical theory, though it is rarely credited to Arendt and tends to lack the kind of interrelated concepts we see in Arendt's political thought. For example, in his famous *Pedagogy of the Oppressed*, Paolo Freire writes, "Human beings are not built in silence, but in word, in work, in action—reflection . . . no one can say a true word alone—nor can she say it for another, in a prescriptive act which robs others of their words" (25). bell hooks, heavily influenced by Freire, opens her work *Teaching to Transgress* with a famous inscription from Freire that encapsulates Arendtian beliefs about action—even as entwined with work—and brushes against notions of life process perhaps even more succinctly: "'to begin always anew, to make, to reconstruct, and to not spoil, to refuse to bureaucratize the mind, to understand and to live life as a process—live to become'" (hooks 1). Freire's rhetoric "to begin always anew" certainly sounds as if it is right out of Arendt; she used this exact language nearly two decades prior to his first writing.

Despite these preliminary connections, in fact Arendt's concepts are not an initially easy model for thinking about classrooms, about teaching, and certainly about graduate student teachers, those wayward souls located in the precarious position of being both teacher and student. In part, Arendtian thought poses difficulty because when we start to categorize what teachers do, we tend to run into overlaps that make such categorization messy. On first glance, the classroom seems an arena for "appearances" on the part of teacher and student, and surely teachers, in participation with students, "work" in the sense that they routinely create a kind of lasting record of instruction through syllabi, assignments, grades, and even instructional strategies or lesson concepts. However, as soon as we start to sort these activities, we run into questions. Is a great assignment only an example of work, or—once implemented and thus unpredictable—does it become a catalyst for action? Does action happen only when the teacher spontaneously abandons a planned lesson, or can a tried-and-true lesson idea evolve and renew itself over multiple attempts? Would that make it a form of action or just an effective tool of the fabrication process? Further—and perhaps more important—how does our experimentation with these Arendtian concepts help us to better understand the experiences of graduate students who must learn how to teach writing? In trying on these connected, though distinct, theoretical concepts, we discover just how layered, conflicted, and instructive graduate students' first formulations of writing pedagogy can be. Accordingly, in what follows I not only explore the meaning gained when graduate students' experiences seem clearly representative of either work or action but also follow the overlapping threads and honor the codependency of Arendt's concepts. The following discussion moves back and forth between action and work, never dealing with the two concepts as entirely separate ideas but always in terms of each other.

Arendt's sparse writing on schooling only further complicates our analysis. In his recent essay "Human Conditions for Teaching: The Place of Pedagogy in Arendt's Vita Activa," Christopher Higgins's project is a daunting one: he maintains that Arendt's concept of action is a relevant and useful model for thinking about classrooms while also contending with the fact that Arendt herself has argued elsewhere that action has no place in school. Throughout this chapter, I draw on two major pieces of Higgins's discussion in order to demonstrate how the graduate students in this study integrated Arendtian action and work into their first semester experiences. First, Higgins questions the limitations Arendt puts on action and thus her reasoning behind its inappropriateness for school; second, Higgins offers a reformulated model for action—in conjunction with work—that allows both to serve usefully as a theoretical "middle space" between teaching and learning. I find this notion of "middle space" quite relevant not only to the relationship between action and work but also to the positioning of the graduate students in this study who found themselves at once teacher and student.

In her essay "The Crisis in Education," Arendt responds to what she sees as a model of schooling designed to make students—and Arendt is particularly thinking about children here—into political actors before they are ready. School, for Arendt, is not the place where students should be asked to "appear before others" as actors do. Such self- revelation necessitates a mature enough relationship to oneself and to the world—and all its problems—to risk self-disclosure and take responsibility for being a "who" that enacts change. Referencing young Hamlet's burden of a world "out of joint," Arendt explains the role of school in preparing actors to "set it right":

> We are always educating for a world that is or is becoming out of joint, for this is the basic human situation. . . . Because the world is made by mortals, it wears out; and because it continuously changes its inhabitants, it runs the risk of becoming as mortal as they. To preserve the world against the mortality of its creators and inhabitants, it must be constantly set right anew. The problem is simply to educate in such a way that a setting-right remains actually possible, even though it can, of course, never be assured. Our hope always hangs on the new which every generation brings; but precisely because we can base our hope only on this, we destroy everything if we so try to control the new that we, the old, can dictate how it will

look. Exactly for the sake of what is new and revolutionary in every child, education must be conservative; it must preserve this newness and introduce it as a new thing into an old world. ("Crisis" 192–93; qtd. in Higgins 420)

The challenge here is to understand the extent to which, if at all, teachers can also be actors and the classroom space can somehow be an arena for such action, beyond the sheltering role Arendt seems to assign it. This challenge is particularly important when we think of graduate student writing teachers, since they operate as teachers and as students: they are at a university not only to study, say, Victorian poetry but also, arguably, to learn *how* to teach writing while they also teach writing. In other words, while they function as teachers in classrooms, they are equally functioning as students, learners who need to understand what it means to teach writing in the context of the larger university and also in terms of the constantly evolving scholarly field(s) of composition and rhetoric. Building on Higgins's intellectual project, I asked the following questions of the graduate student teachers in this study: Do teachers act in the Arendtian sense of the term? To what extent might learning be a form of action? Just how protected should graduate students be, as they are, after all, "grown ups," though certainly students, nonetheless? Finally, what are the contours and particular problems of the "old world" they inherit when introduced to composition as a field? How might graduate student writing teachers—when handed their quickly-becoming-outdated world of first-year writing in the university—set it right?

Because school, for Arendt, protects its students from the glaring reality of the public, there is a kind of betrayal involved in asking students to stake out a public, political identity before they are ready.[1] Arendt argues that the "tyranny of the peer group" that ensues when school no longer offers some protection from the space of public appearances "can have the ill-effect of fixing a being in place, freezing the development of someone 'who is in process of becoming but not yet complete'" (qtd. in Higgins 426). Higgins acknowledges the potential damages that Arendt fears and then argues for a classroom that serves as a kind of mediating space for action where, much like the theatrical stage, students—and, consequently, teacher—can try on different roles without being permanently contained in any one. In this sense, students are offered some degree of protection while also being prepared for the participatory, collaborative public arena. Higgins asks that we consider more fully the teacher's role in facilitating this "middle space" as a kind of action: "Here is a place, the teacher says, where your words will have weight but where you may also write your story in pencil" (435). I find Higgins's metaphor very relevant for new graduate student writing teachers, who are unquestionably still "in process," not yet ready to be actors but also very much in need of a mediating space for practice.

The mediating space of the classroom is dependent upon a blending of Arendt's concepts of work and action. Higgins argues that Arendt herself allows for this flexibility in her own treatment of these concepts. He explains, "Work is an example of kinesis—a process that aims at something outside itself, the attainment of which masks its completion—whereas action fits the model of energia, as an activity that contains its aim within itself" (437). Given the goals of the classroom to introduce and present "what we have tried and done, asked and found, sought and avoided," teaching then "represents a kind of hermeneutical gray zone between kinesis and energia" (437). Pointing to Arendt's own valuing of the American founding and, in particular, the drafting of the Constitution, which she discusses in, among other works, *On Revolution*, Higgins argues that this is a fine example of a similar gray zone, where there is mediation and augmentation, a collaboration between action and work. Writing, for Arendt, is typically confined to the capacity of work as it creates a record of actors' accomplishments. However, Arendt argues that the writing of the Constitution represents action since the document—in order to be what it is—must be continuously renewed and augmented for the sake of bringing together successive generations. Without this capacity for renewal, the revolutionary spirit of the American founding would have died with the Founders—remembered, perhaps, but not renewed. This overlap, for Higgins, parallels the role of the teacher, who not only occupies a mediating space, the classroom, but also must continuously augment information—in this case, the curriculum—in the practice of teaching. This juncture, defined by mediation and augmentation, Higgins argues, exemplifies Arendtian action for the classroom while underscoring its codependency on work.

I draw on Higgins's reformulation of Arendt to demonstrate the diversity of experience and varying levels of preparedness on the part of the graduate students in this study. Amid their many early pedagogical encounters, these new teacher/students confirm for us the perils of being thrust into the public arena too soon and also demonstrate their own sensitivities to the peer pressures that tend to dominate in such a situation. However, at their best, they also showcase the possibilities of mediation and augmentation, suggesting a kind of middle ground that might best fit the precarious task of being both teacher and student, as contained in two classroom spaces: first-year writing and graduate school. This is accomplished only through a kind of blending of Arendtian action and work. As we identify these most exemplary moments that operate in a middle space, drawing on and also augmenting Arendt's concepts, we can better design approaches to the support and preparation of graduate student writing teachers.

TESS ON THE STAND VS. PHILOSOPHY PHIL: TEACHERS, STUDENTS, AND THE PUBLIC REALM

Our first task is to understand, in its lived form, Arendt's conviction about the dangers of pushing a being "in process" forward into the glaring light of the public before he or she is ready. Tess's early experiences in the classroom, which spurred her more deeply toward a teaching practice founded on laboring alone, stand as a preliminary example of the potential consequences of a premature public appearance. As discussed in the previous chapter, Tess suffered serious public pressure at the hand of a particularly disruptive and challenging student, "Philosophy Phil," as well as a kind of whole-class revolt over her grading practices. She explained her growing anxiety about being questioned in public: "Because of my inexperience, I already lack confidence; if I say I don't know, then I might as well sit down and let the students run the class. I feel like I have to know the answer, or my students won't respect me; they'll lose faith in me and this class" (email, 1 Oct.). Tess seemed to understand herself here quite clearly: she did not have experience; she lacked confidence; she was, as Arendt might say, "in process." However, because of her teaching responsibilities, she also worried about the consequences her status might have on the class and on her role as "teacher."

When students staged a "revolt" after she graded their first papers quite harshly, Tess was challenged to come up with answers—to take a kind of position on the course—that she did not actually have: "They were so critical and skeptical of the course and the inconsistencies in the program. So it was also critical of me—they asked, 'How is your system beneficial to us? Why are you right?'" (email, 20 Sept.). As discussed in chapter 2, Tess's response to this level of public demand and scrutiny was to enter into a kind of endless grading and conferencing process; her approach to teaching aligned dangerously with Arendtian labor alone, where Tess dedicated her effort—and her emerging understanding of how writing is taught—to mere survival and repetition.

For his part, Philosophy Phil's public confrontations with Tess, which quickly became a classroom norm, both embarrassed and undermined her. She was consistently nervous for class, knowing he'd be there and worried he'd challenge her publicly. In mid-October, Phil took his threatening presence to a new level. He turned in a paper with a disturbing drawing and written message on the front cover. Tess described the incident in an email:

> I collected papers today from the students and his had a very disturbing drawing on the cover. It was a cartoon of a tiger (?) holding out his tongue while smoking a cigarette and shooting himself in the head with a gun (shows gun, head wound, and bullet exiting from the other side). The note by Phil reads: "Ms. ——, As someone who considers himself both a student and a teacher, this paper insults us both! You have succeeded in sending me off the deep end of epistemology. Just look at what you did! Shame on you!—'Pistol' Phil, Squad Leader, 187th Infantry Regiment (AASLT)." (17 Oct.)

It is difficult to make clear sense of Phil's intentions, or the meaning behind his drawing and words. If he was trying to intimidate, he succeeded brilliantly. His actions thoroughly frightened Tess and brought the task of "teacher" to a staggering new level. Phil's self-description, as "someone who considers himself both a student and a teacher," is confusing and suggests perhaps a misperception (or delusional perception) of his own status and power. He blamed Tess for "sending" him "off the deep end of epistemology" and then linked these words with the suicidal picture—the tiger character in the drawing was literally blowing his brains out with frustration. Perhaps Phil underestimated the impact this drawing and message would have on his young female teacher? Perhaps he thought she'd see humor in it? Or, perhaps he intended to instill fear and intimidation?

Whatever Phil's intentions, the effects of his actions were immediate on Tess. After describing Phil's paper, she expressed her exasperation: "This is my first semester of graduate school, my first experience, (ever!), of teaching—why do I have to deal with this? It's not fair. Now I am sick, worried, completely freaked out—how am I supposed to concentrate on my own studies?" (email, 17 Oct.). This problem student had a decisive upper hand. Tess was, in many ways, frozen at the moment she confronted Phil's paper. Her interest in teaching, composition as a discipline, and her own graduate coursework faltered significantly. Her only escape from this state was the FYWP administration; she went immediately in hopes of removing Phil from her class and having him appropriately punished.

The first administrative response was to remove Phil from Tess's class, report him to the university disciplinary committee, and offer him one-on-one tutoring so that he could complete his credits by the end of the semester. Phil was assured that, should there be any further problems, he would lose the course credit altogether. However, Tess felt that the one-on-one tutoring was more of a privilege than a punishment. She wrote, angrily, "How is this fair to the other students? Students who could benefit from one-on-one writing instruction and deserve it more . . . guess I should just be content with the fact that he is out of my class, but somehow because I feel so personally violated, I want justice, man! How dare he? He should be kicked off the planet!" (email, 29 Oct.). In this scenario, Tess felt personally betrayed by the administration. Although she argued that Phil's disciplinary consequences were not "fair to the other students . . . who could benefit from one-on-one writing instruction," she took Phil's fate as a personal affront. The FYWP's relatively soft treatment of Phil, in Tess's eyes, marked an ugly schism between the university and Tess. This was particularly poignant in her case, as Tess had completed her undergraduate work at Public U and returned for her doctorate with significant loyalty to the school.

While Tess initially sought refuge in administrative authorities, ultimately the FYWP's handling of the situation only pushed Tess further into the public spotlight she had come to so fear. She was soon notified that she would be needed to testify as a witness at Phil's disciplinary hearing, a public event that was a university-level response to his behavior. Immediately, Tess felt further betrayed by the FYWP. Initially, the administration had confronted Phil and left Tess out of things, to protect and comfort her: "The FYWP did such a great job of removing me from the situation by saying THEY came across the paper and THEY had a problem with it, and that is how it was presented to Phil. Now I have to walk in and say, no, I was the one who showed it to them, I'm the one who feels uncomfortable with it" (email, 26 Nov.). With this move, Tess found she was threatened anew, publicly exposed to the student who had so humiliated and intimidated her. She felt she "no longer [had] the protection FYWP gave me by taking it out of my hands" (email, 17 Oct.). She had to face Phil, as well as university administrators, and publicly name her fear, her discomfort, and her intimidation. She had to identify Phil's actions as effective and powerful. She resented the entire situation and felt that, by testifying, she would revisit feelings she'd worked hard to overcome: "I was so angry that he [Phil] could make me feel hopeless and loathsome toward my experience here, and now I have to grapple with those feelings again" (email, 26 Nov.).

Tess's frustration increased as the disciplinary hearing approached, particularly because "no one really knows, either, what exactly happens at the hearing." Feeling a renewed sense of fear, Tess desperately

wanted to know just what to expect from the experience. Furthermore, that she had "all males . . . to turn to for guidance on this
situation" on the administrative level at Public U was an added
frustration because "they just don't get it!" She explained, "They
don't understand how Phil made me FEEL—how uncomfortable
and threatening the environment he created was. Why? Why do I
have to be there?" (email, 26 Nov.). Tess did not offer further insight
into why or how her gender played into her feelings of vulnerability
and discomfort, though surely many women have felt similarly. The
absence of a female administrator convinced Tess that the administration could not properly understand the gravity of the situation.
Only her testimony stood to convey the reality of her experience,
from her vantage point, though the mere thought of facing Phil
publicly was an overwhelming stressor.

The day of public testimony finally arrived in early December.
This means that the "Phil situation" was drawn out for the length
of Tess's first semester, beginning with his challenging comments
in class and ending with her taking the stand. Tess's account of the
disciplinary hearing began with the admission, "Yesterday was probably the worst thing I have gone through in my life." Tess described
the experience accordingly:

> As soon as I was in the room, face to face with him again, I
> just started to cry, even though I was trying so hard not to.
> The initial investigator offered to go outside with me so I could
> calm down, and he explained the process to me. He told me
> not to worry about "nailing Phil to the wall," I should just say
> how I felt. Even when I was called on, there was a brief moment
> where I started to cry again, and I thought I wouldn't make it
> through, but I was able to keep it together. After I was done,
> [the FYWP director] came over to me and told me that I was
> amazing, which felt really good. (email, 4 Dec.)

Tess's emotionality was significant when "face to face with him
again" because it represented an honest and public communication
of her experience. Her crying was an admission of the very real effect this problem student had on her as a teacher, a woman, and a

person. That Tess was finally "able to keep it together" meant that, in addition to expressing herself emotionally, she was also able to make verbally clear the details of Phil's classroom behavior and its impact on her and the rest of the class. That the FYWP director approached her following her testimony and told her that she was "amazing" was an acknowledgment from someone who witnessed Tess's public (and personal) sharing. It was an affirmation, for Tess, of her public persona, "which felt really good."

However, the compliment did not prevent negative after-effects of Tess's public exposure. She admitted to feeling bruised and some-what used by the university in the days following the ordeal. She wrote in an email, "Everything felt so fucked up. I didn't want to be there, I didn't want to ever come back, and I started to blame the University for putting me in this position." Finally, Tess posed the question to me, "How am I supposed to be a normal teacher, a normal student, normal person after all of this?" (email, 4 Dec.). At this point, I responded by asking her to clarify what she meant by "normal," to which I received the following response:

> I guess what I mean about feeling "normal" again is wondering if I will be able to walk into a classroom at the beginning of the semester without thinking, "Okay, which one of these students is Phil?" I am wondering whether I even want to walk into any more classrooms at all. I am wondering whether I want to continue at Public U. As I try to write my final papers, I find myself not caring about the subject matter, not caring about the professors or the classes, not caring about passing or failing, just not caring about being here. I feel like Public U screwed me over this semester, and have no interest in giving anything back. I'm beaten down and exhausted. I want to believe that all I need is winter break but I don't know. I just don't know how to feel about all this. (email, 7 Dec.)

Perhaps Tess's holding the university responsible was not so much a move to blame the administration for putting Phil in her class, which, surely, was mere chance, but rather a kind of frustration at the practice of putting her—a new graduate student who had never taught before—in charge at all. Her impulse to blame Public U here was Tess's active response to a situation that made her feel largely powerless; afraid of the student who troubled her, she turned with greater confidence and resentment toward the university she had always embraced and at which she previously felt at home.

It is at this juncture that we must return to Arendt's advocacy for school as a kind of protective space for future actors. The administrative authority Tess thought should have protected her had, in the end, only pushed her further out front. Given the teacher/student balancing act negotiated by all graduate student writing teachers, Tess seemed to have tipped too far toward a claiming of her role or identity as "teacher" when what she was most feeling was her inexperience and her lack of confidence, which she associated with the fact that she was in many ways still—even mostly—a student. But whose student and whose teacher was she? The FYWP's decision to have her testify at Phil's disciplinary hearing suggests that the administration saw her less as one of "their" graduate students and perhaps more fully as one of their instructors; after all, she was the teacher in Phil's class. In this moment, Tess's studenthood was defined perhaps exclusively by her concurrent pursuit of a doctorate in literature. However, if we think of Tess not only as a teacher for the FYWP but also—as a first-time teacher new to the discipline, program, and curriculum—as a student of the FYWP, we are left to explore Arendt's anxieties about premature action and her contention that school must be protective.

An appropriately mediated space—one that invites students to experiment with representations of the world (and here, of course, Arendt draws on Plato's cave allegory)—makes the experience of "studenthood" a desirable preparation for the "real" world one day. However, in Tess we heard defeat, "not caring about the subject matter, not caring about the professors or the classes, not caring about passing or failing." Her sense of herself as a student at Public U was no longer realistic, almost as if the experience of the disciplinary hearing cut off her access to that aspect of her identity. Tess's language of exhaustion here echoes Arendt's prediction in "The Crisis in Education" about the dire consequences involved when school ceases to be a mediating, protective space and students are asked to be actors before they are ready:

> The same destruction of the real living space occurs wherever the attempt is made to turn the children themselves into a kind of world. Among these peer groups then arises a public life of a sort and, quite apart from the fact that is it not a real one and that the whole attempt is a sort of fraud, the damaging fact remains that children—that is, human beings in process of becoming but not yet complete—are thereby forced to expose themselves to the light of a public existence. (187)

My interest here is not in putting graduate students—adults, surely—into the category of children but rather in allowing them the right, it seems to me, to be "in process of becoming but not yet complete" as writing teachers. While I might argue that this notion of being "in process" is an apt one for all teachers, however experienced, graduate student teachers seem especially deserving of the time and space to work on "becoming." The consequences, for Tess, of this denial were quite staggering, and she appeared to suffer from an arrested development of sorts, resentful of the authorities she trusted and robbed of her own identification with learning.

Arendt recognizes that sometimes actors err, and for this she allows for the faculty of forgiving, where we release each other from infractions that occur in the public world. Arendt explains in *The Human Condition*, "But trespassing is an everyday occurrence which is in the very nature of action's constant establishment of new relationships within a web of relations, and it needs forgiving, dismissing, in order to make it possible for life to go on by constantly releasing men from what they have done unknowingly" (197). While Tess had the option of forgiving all involved—Philosophy Phil, the FYWP—for her negative experiences, she seemed unconvinced that the FYWP had acted "unknowingly" in some ways and, more broadly, appeared too scarred to go forward, to be willing to either act or be acted upon again. In the Arendtian sense, then, Tess removed herself from the world; she no longer wished to contribute to its regeneration. There was no denying her bravery in testifying against Philosophy Phil, of course, but complicated questions remain about whether her student status should have overridden her status as teacher, where some greater degree of sheltering would have better nurtured her toward becoming the teacher she ultimately aspired to be during that first semester. Perhaps, had Tess been "ready" to function publicly as an actor—to claim her responsibility for the class, her identity as the teacher, and her status as FYWP representative—she would have been equally ready to forgive the transgressions. Her evident bruising, at least at the end of the first semester, suggests that she was "in process" but also "not yet." Tess's experiences in this case and her response to them are not representative of Arendt's ideal notion of action but rather stand as an example of Arendt's worries about acting too soon: when we ask others to say who they are before they know themselves, the result is resentment and ambiguity.

SILENCING PEER PRESSURE: RESISTING THE "BITCH AND MOAN"

In what she sees as an overexposed and fraudulent "world," Arendt argues that peer pressure dominates when beings in process are pushed to act before they are ready. The swell and influence of the peer group is felt most profoundly by those least prepared to resist it, surely, and the authenticity of action is sacrificed. Nancy operated as a fascinating figure in this study for her awareness of this very phenomenon as it exists among graduate students struggling through their first semesters, her decision to stay silent for much of the semester rather than participate in what she saw as negative group thinking, and her subsequent—and very vocal—design of a teacher persona in response. Each piece of Nancy's experience here represented a changing relationship to her role as an actor, as well as an effort to carve out a very distinctive middle position between teacher and student, one that was much in line with Higgins's reformulation of Arendtian action for the classroom.

Throughout my semester-long interaction with study participants, Nancy stood out as the one who consulted me the least; she appeared to be the least involved in the project. While the other participants sent me a steady flow of emails worrying about one thing or another,

Nancy emailed me only when I asked for a response about something. At our monthly group get-togethers, she distinguished herself with her reticence, not her outspokenness. I attributed this reserve, initially, to two possibilities: either she simply wasn't as interested in my study, or she just didn't feel she needed as much advice and support as the other three participants.

When I finally asked Nancy to explain her semester-long silence during an exit interview at the end of the first semester, she described her very conflicted identity between teacher and student and her sense of alienation from the scholarly goals of her fellow graduate students:

> I don't really know what I'm doing here and I'm not really a literature person, and I don't know if I feel like reading anymore. . . . I get so frustrated listening to people bitch and moan about everything—about how they have to teach, and they shouldn't be teaching when they came here to study—what the hell do you think you're going to do with the rest of your life? Not all of us will work at Harvard and be able to write books . . . and you are going to alienate an entire generation of students because you don't care about teaching? I get so tired of listening to people complain—they complain about the practicum—like how could you go through your graduate career and not learn how to teach? It's pretty amazing to me that academics could dismiss all the other people in the world—where teaching them is such a chore. It's really frustrating. So, I'd like to teach at a community college. . . . Half the time I think I should just become a high school teacher because . . . I want to teach and I want normal people to be able to appreciate writing and literature. (exit interview)

For Arendt, Nancy's self-disclosure fits with her traditional notion of action as "natality," where "with word and deed we insert ourselves into the human world and this insertion is like a second birth" (*Human Condition* 176). However, Nancy's words also underscore her break from Arendt, as she offers an explanation for many weeks of near-speechlessness. Are we to value only her diatribe? Or is there some space for understanding—as action—the identity

Nancy equally staked out in silence? And perhaps more important, how do Nancy's silence and her speech help us to better understand the role and purpose of Arendtian action in the writing classroom? Nancy's silence matters because it asks us to rethink the traditional notion of action—"words and deeds"—that Arendt values and to consider the idea that silence, too, is a "deed" and one that can speak forcibly. Nancy's extended period of speechlessness finds meaningful connection in Cheryl Glenn's work on rhetorical silence and ultimately suggests that perhaps—in addition to "hearing out" new writing teachers—we also need to learn to read and listen for what they may leave unsaid. According to Glenn, "silence reveals speech at the same time that it enacts its own sometimes complimentary rhetoric" (3). Glenn goes on to explore the distinctions and overlap between enacting silence and being silenced, noting the power ultimately wielded by both. In Nancy's case, her choice of silence was a kind of ideological resistance to attitudes about teaching and the university. However, in her resistance, she inevitably underscored the complicated, ambiguous, and disjointed relationship between new writing teachers and the institutionalized role of first-year writing. Nancy's silence was an effort to reject and distance herself from this larger institutional context; however, as many WPAs will admit, such effort is fraught with difficulty for new writing teachers.

Nancy's rhetorical act of silence represents a double-sided, paradoxically significant facet of the unspoken that has roots in resistance and control. Glenn explains, "Sociocultural silences include the locational silences of the courtroom, classroom, library, prison, church, and hospital. And such silences also inhabit acts of protest and control. In those ways, silence is used to preserve ideologies of all kinds" (18). Nancy's silence was an act of both protest and control, though this significance did not become clear until the exit interview. In her choice to be silent for most of the semester, Nancy protested against what she perceived to be the other graduate students' negative attitudes about teaching and students. Her silence, too, was an effort to preserve her own belief systems about the importance of teaching and her valuing of students' "real lives" against what she viewed as detached, overly academic reading and writing assignments.

But as Glenn's words suggest, protest, control, and the preservation of ideologies are enacted by institutions on individuals, too. In the first-year writing context, the often-fraught politics around the first-year course requirement position many graduate and adjunct instructors to espouse course objectives over which they feel no sense of ownership. Accordingly, new graduate and part-time writing teachers may question the validity of the first-year writing requirement, and teaching against the backdrop of such questioning—particularly when their questions find no place of easy welcome—creates a kind of teacherly authority that is unstable and unwanted. In her critique of the first-year writing requirement, Sharon Crowley writes: "The required first-year course still serves American universities as a border checkpoint, the institutional site wherein students either provide proper identification or retreat to wherever they came from. In America's cultural imagination, mastery of 'correct' English still signifies that its users are suitable to the class of educated persons" (231). Nancy's resistance was inspired, in part, by her sense of disconnect from the "goals" for student learning articulated in foundational composition scholarship, which she read in the teaching practicum course, and from the students she faced in class whom she identified as outside of a privileged, "educated" class. If we follow Crowley's critique, Nancy seemed saddled with the task of university gatekeeper, a task she fundamentally rejected. Nancy and her graduate student colleagues were reluctant, even confused, representatives of a discipline, university, and academic culture to which they didn't fully subscribe.

Reflecting on the difficult work of WPAs in bridging this apparent divide, Bonnie Kyburz calls for integration of new teachers' resistances and questioning. Drawing on Glenn's work on rhetorical silence, Kyburz argues for a move away from "the delineating action of a 'mission statement' or set of desired 'outcomes'" (77). She proposes, instead, that we learn how to "hear" new writing teachers like Nancy: "We may see a new community of knowledgeable peers who communicate insights . . . by listening, by enacting silence in ways that encourage further reflection, by avoiding the temptation to resolve problems in a Q&A format that cannot fully account for the various aspects of a teacher's concern or problem" (77). In Kyburz's call, we are able to witness the double-sided significance of Nancy's silence, which was at once a protest against existing conditions and a preservation of her own beliefs. Nancy's rhetorical performance is also, for Kyburz, a model practice for WPAs and practicum instructors who wish to turn the preparation of new writing teachers into collective, complex work.

In giving equal attention to Nancy's silence, we ultimately must explore what (or who) is lost when we read through Arendt's valuing of "words and deeds" alone. In her silence, Nancy resisted the peer pressure so characteristic, for Arendt, of the fraudulent "world" that we cultivate when schools—and students—are pushed prematurely into the arena of action. We can understand Nancy's silence as an acknowledgment that perhaps, all along, she was aware of her peers' (and her own) lack of preparedness to occupy a clear position—teacher—when she finally says, "How could you go through your graduate career and not learn how to teach?" In other words, Nancy argued that she, and the others, needed to learn and therefore had no business complaining about, for example, the required practicum course designed to help them do just that. Nancy thus chose not to complain, to be silent, in an effort to define herself in terms of her needs as a learner, as someone who was "almost but not yet." Further, given her "fledgling" status, Nancy took the position that she was fortunate to be teaching at all: after all, she still had so much to learn and yet "got the job" anyway.

Does Nancy's staking out a self-definition as "in between" teacher and student, between speech and especially silence, resonate with Arendt's prized words and deeds? In Higgins's discussion of Arendt on education, "the world appears in school only in a mediated way," which requires "both exposure to the workings of the world and protection from having to make this debut too early" (426). In Nancy, we recognize a desire for mediation, an acceptance of the practicum course as needed support, and a willingness to incur the growing pains of early teaching. In this way, she seemed to think of herself as a student, primarily, even as she made her way as a teacher. Her approach to teaching, then, was defined by her own experience of studenthood and her sense that she, along with her students, operated in a mediated space, one that was preparatory for the world-out-there, though perhaps not yet fully in it. Nancy's rejection of her peers' complaints seemed also an indictment of what she saw as their reluctance to occupy such a mediated space. She asked, "What the hell do you think you're going to do with the rest of your life? Not all of us will work at Harvard and be able to write books." With these words, Nancy questioned what she saw as her peers' dismissal of teaching writing—and also of learning how to teach writing—as elitist and shortsighted.

It is, of course, possible that Nancy's peers complained not because they felt they were "above" teaching writing but rather because they valued a teacher-as-authority-figure approach that might disallow the kind of mediated space that Nancy embraced and, whether desirable or not, proved impossible to achieve in the first semester of teaching. For example, recall Tess's sense of inadequacy when confronted with her students' angry demands, "'How is your system beneficial to us? Why are you right?'" That her answer, in truth, was "I don't know" convinced Tess that "I might as well sit down and let the students run the class. . . . They'll lose faith in me and this class." Far from considering herself a kind of intellectual elite who never planned to stoop as low as the first-year writing classroom, Tess instead seemed anxious and insecure about her "imposter" status in the classroom and considered a teacher who simply "doesn't know" not a teacher at all. She did not allow herself to be a student, since only in perverse, failed classrooms would "the students run the class."

The contrast between Nancy's feelings of gratitude and good fortune for her teaching assignment and her peers' resentment, for whatever reasons, continues to present an interesting paradox. While Nancy, herself a twenty-three-year-old graduate of a prestigious university, likely sensed her personal difference from the diverse, often nontraditional students in her evening composition class, she was also at odds with her graduate studies and many of her graduate student colleagues. She explained: "I mostly feel alienated from my fellow grad students. I don't mind so much, because I don't really feel like I have a lot in common with most of them. I have a lot more in common with my students, and with the people I tutor—I am trying to juggle a million different things and I am struggling to get by" (email, 14 Jan.). Nancy's point of connection with her students—"I am trying to juggle a million things and I am struggling to get by"—seemed to her an honest representation of the reality of her situation as teacher and graduate student. These roles, for Nancy, were equally defined by "struggle" and thus gave her a kind of permission to define herself, while assigned the role of "teacher" by the university, as just as much a "student" in the classroom as her first-year writing students. She discussed this configuration in light of her own sense of self:

> I am not very comfortable with myself in a lot of ways, but all I really want is to be appreciated for trying. I try to appreciate my students for trying because they are all interesting people. So, my acting like I am one of my students isn't really an intentional act—I really do feel like one of them. And half the time, I don't really understand why they have to learn certain things that I am teaching them, but I try to admit it as I work through it because if I don't they will see right through me anyway. (email, 14 Jan.)

With this explanation, Nancy highlighted the complex and layered role of the teacher as one who must prepare students for a world beyond the immediate classroom, even as she admitted that she felt great uncertainty about the curriculum: "I don't really understand why they have to learn certain things that I am teaching them."

Nancy's conflicted status here points us to tension between and dependency on Arendt's concepts of work and action, as well as to her insistence on the mediating role of school. In vocalizing her concerns and resistance in the exit interview, Nancy appeared the quintessential Arendtian actor. However, in her connection to her own student status, her reluctance to take a position of clear authority, and her admitted confusion over the "materials" of the course—the syllabus, reading and writing assignments, grading standards—Nancy raised questions about the "lasting products" Arendt's workers create that are meant to immortalize action. The idea of Arendtian fabrication, "whose sum constitutes the human artifice," is suddenly in need of revision. When we take seriously the contributions of new graduate student writing teachers, we must explore a classroom product—in pedagogical approach and in the "stuff" of the composition class— borne of conflict. Such conflict positions Nancy, and other graduate students assigned the task of teaching writing, in a clear middle space between action and work, between invention and fabrication, and between teacher and student. Simple dichotomies do not work. This may be our most valuable lesson from the study of new graduate students' classrooms, one that stretches far beyond their confines. In what follows, I assess Nancy's formulation of a teaching practice, as well as her discussion of assigned readings and the pressure of grading, as a saving force against the pressures of being swept into an arena for which she knew she was not ready. While Tess seemed unable to resist this premature push into action's public arena and thus spiraled into a teaching practice consumed by laboring, Nancy claimed a safe space from which to fight back.

Nancy's identification with her students, central to this notion of a kind of safe, middle space, was furthered by her discomfort with the level of difficulty and, at times, highly intellectual stance of the selected readings on the assigned syllabus. Antonio Gramsci's essay "The Intellectuals" from *Prison Notebooks* was a stumbling point for many first-year undergraduates; students of all the study participants complained about the reading. Nancy explained to me that the Gramsci piece was too disconnected from students' lives: "I want my students to express themselves and make connections with the outside world. When a forty year-old woman who's struggling to get her degree in nursing has to read Gramsci . . . it's bullshit. I'd rather have her write an essay on anything" (exit interview). Here, Nancy's assertion that the student should "write an essay on anything" at first suggests that anything other than Gramsci might be more useful for the student. However, on further consideration, Nancy's words also imply that it is an "outside world" that determines what her student needs, though it is not clear if this outside world is of her own imagining or informed by her student. Still, Nancy takes on a role here familiar to Arendt's ideas about schooling: teachers are "representatives of a world for which they must assume responsibility although they themselves did not make it, and even though they may, secretly or openly, wish it were other than it is" (Arendt, *Human Condition* 189). In Nancy's world—or, more correctly, in the "outside world" for which she had the task of preparing a forty-year-old nursing student—Gramsci was irrelevant. Her anxiety and resentment toward the FYWP was based upon a disagreement over what first-year writing students need if they are to be prepared for this world. Of course, questions remain: Why can't this "world" include the academic life beyond the first-year writing course? Wasn't Nancy's task, in part, to prepare her nursing student to succeed in other college-level courses? In what ways might her rejection of Gramsci be an unfair move to speak for a student who, clearly, was pursuing the intellectual work of an undergraduate degree? In other words, why did Nancy get to decide that her student had no use for Gramsci? While these questions do not have easy answers, they do point most importantly to Nancy's reluctance to present herself, publicly, as the teacher when she found the materials of the course a misrepresentation of the outside world for which she felt she had to prepare her students.

Nancy's discomfort with the assigned readings for her first-year students highlighted her dissatisfaction with the materials of her own graduate instruction, readings in foundational composition scholarship required by the practicum syllabus. Nancy attributed the FYWP's rationale for including difficult texts on the syllabus to the philosophy of David Bartholomae, whose important works "Inventing the University" and "The Tidy House: Basic Writing in the American Curriculum" were required reading on the practicum syllabus during Nancy's first semester. When I asked her to make clear her reference to Bartholomae, she explained that she understood his philosophy as "Read really difficult texts to improve." She went on to further clarify, "The students who were having a really difficult time were put through it unnecessarily. [They were] mimicking university speak and not doing a good job. I know a struggling student will probably get there and that's fine, but . . . I just feel that students should develop their own voice first" (exit interview). Further, Nancy contended that her students' struggle with writing was inseparable from the chasm between the demands of their lives in the outside world and the assigned syllabus readings:

> I really think that a lot of their mistakes come out of their own lack of motivation more than their inability to write. Maybe this is an assumption I am making, but I do think that if my students were more interested in what we were reading, they would write better essays. Only a handful of my students struggle with the act of writing itself. (email, 26 Oct.)

Nancy drew a clear dividing line between the writing that first-year students need to do and the kind of writing defined for them by composition scholarship. Because Nancy attributed the uninspiring readings for the first-year course to the recommendations made in her own readings in composition theory, her frustrations with her graduate studies were suddenly on a collision course with those of her first-year writing students. In Nancy's view, both were assigned readings that failed to resonate in their "worlds." The required teaching practice course thus served as a space where issues of practice, theory, and university requirements collided for Nancy.

This collision course yielded an instructional style defined by Nancy's occupation of a middle space between teacher and student. She created a kind of "we're all in this together" teaching approach in which both she and her students struggled with texts with which they did not find easy connection. As a classroom observer, I witnessed Nancy's tendency, in her interaction with her students, to "admit it"—that she didn't "really understand why they have to learn certain things that I am teaching them"—"as I work through it" when I visited her evening composition class. The class was discussing Gramsci, of course, and Nancy was very vocal in questioning the usefulness of the text. Her questions hinted at the answers she expected: "Why was Gramsci hard? Why would someone in the working class not understand it? Could anything in this essay apply to your position?" Students responded accordingly with negative answers, such as, "Well, I really don't understand why we had to read it at all." As she asked these questions, I noted in my observation log that she remained seated, did not use the board, and in general portrayed an attitude that was both "very subdued" and "funny, in a sarcastic kind of way" (Nancy, author's observation notes). Nancy's body language, her display of reluctance toward the Gramsci reading, and her negative style of questioning matched behavior more typical of a student than a teacher. She posited herself more as a reluctant student assigned to do a class presentation than as a teacher taking responsibility for a class and curriculum. In many ways, I believe this is a more accurate portrayal of how she produced an instructional model in the first semester. She was a student given an assignment: she had to teach a syllabus she did not design and read selections in composition theory for which she did not feel a sense of conviction or agreement.

When we consider Nancy's situation, we must note that she was, in fact, notably concerned with the value of what students learned and what they produced, particularly in relation to the "outside world," as she said. This makes her an important subject in terms of Arendt's notion of work, as Arendt's language indicates a similar desire for products with worldly relevance, "with enough durability to remain in the world as an independent entity," as well as a convincing example of Arendt's ideas about the role of school in preparing future actors (*Human Condition* 143). The viability of her writing classroom—its potential for creating a "lasting product" for student use in the world outside, as well as its appropriateness for grooming future actors, students who would one day participate in that public space outside the more protected classroom—was clearly in jeopardy.

Nancy's move to initiate an alternate teaching practice by radicalizing her presentation of the course materials raises questions about the role of invention and renewal in the fabrication process, which forces us to revisit Arendt to search for some interchangeability in her concepts of action and work. While Arendt typically locates invention within the purview of action, recall her fascination with the American founding and contention that, in fact, the writing of the US Constitution serves as an example of action. This flexibility, as Arendt often argues that writing creates a lasting record of action and thus is an example of work, demonstrates a crucial overlap in these two concepts. Arendt makes an exception for the founding documents because, as Higgins explains, they represent "the creation of an entity whose very durability lay in its constant re-creation" (438). For Higgins, overlap between durability and re-creation finds easy parallel in teaching: "Just as the constitution is a document that expresses natality, required continued augmentation and amendment to be itself . . . the teacher mediates, preserves, and elaborates our cultural constitution" (440). In Nancy's case, we might ask: To what extent might Arendt's worker change the model for the sake of his or her workmanship? Nancy's reconfiguration of a teaching practice as resistant to the materials and goals of the course syllabus seemed to counter any threat of a worker as merely a cog in a larger wheel, not engaged at all with questions about how and what is being made. When workers, in the process of making, reinvent aspects of an inherited model, are they no longer workers but actors? Here we find that Nancy did function much as Higgins's mediator, where the teacher must continually "augment" information in an effort "to find the language through which parts of the past might speak to the present and ideas fashioned in one context might resound in another" (440). Nancy revised an inherited model and repackaged it for students in a way that questioned its very legitimacy. Here she bridged Arendt's concepts of action and work, which signifies the special location of teaching on the "border" of these Arendtian concepts.

While Nancy was able to augment the course's assigned readings by presenting them in a resistant, student-centered style, grading and the merits of grammar instruction posed higher-profile challenges. Nancy continuously questioned her role in grading students' writing, which furthers this idea of an unstable, perhaps constantly changing, "final" product while underscoring the status of a grade as a permanent "record" of a student's classroom performance. Through a required portfolio grading workshop, a memo, and various verbal warnings, the FYWP administration cautioned new TAs against grade inflation. Discussing a portfolio workshop hosted late in the semester by the FYWP, Nancy explained that "now all of a sudden it matters if we screw up because there are grades involved." She pointed out that, despite the "threat from FYWP about possible grade inflation," her assigned mentor "waited such a long time to look at our grading anyway." At the FYWP-hosted portfolio workshop, Nancy felt trapped: "Now what am I supposed to do? Me and Anjel were giving higher grades than anyone else . . . and I felt other people were giving intentionally lower grades because the FYWP was there" (email, 1 Nov.). In this situation, Nancy seemed torn over external pressure from the FYWP, despite the general lack of guidance earlier in the semester and her own convictions about students, their work, and the validity of grading. Ultimately, she refused to grade lower at the portfolio workshop while continuing to feel a sense of conflict over stated programmatic expectations and her own sense of her students' needs and abilities.

Nancy's resistance to existing frameworks for grading practice occasions a rethinking of how she responded to student writing and especially of the relevance of grammar instruction. In an email response to my question "How would you describe the abilities of your students?," Nancy wrote of her professional conflict over issues of grammar, given the message in the practicum course that grammar instruction should not be a primary concern. She explained, "Students struggle with grammar a lot, and it drives me crazy that I am supposed to let it go. I think this is a bad thing in a lot of ways. I think that grammar will help them more in life than writing argumentative essays" (26 Oct.). Again, here we see Nancy's sense of responsibility to students' preparedness for the outside world, to "help them more in life." This commitment was jeopardized for Nancy by her understanding that she was not to focus on grammar, a message she received in the teaching practicum.[2] Because she did not identify with the rationale behind the assigned syllabus and the goals of the course, Nancy augmented the course materials, grading standards, and instructional focus with the conviction that her students' needs did not match those imagined by the FYWP.

The sources of Nancy's personal and professional disconnect signified an estrangement between worker and model, a relationship that Arendt identifies as essential to fabrication. Arendt insists on the "guidance of a model," which the worker must employ to shape

his or her creating; when this model is in jeopardy, of course the
worker, too, is at odds and unlikely to achieve Arendt's lofty goals
for fabrication, which must "transcend both the sheer functionalism
of things produced for consumption and the sheer utility of objects
produced for use" (*Human Condition* 173). Arendt suggests that
"guidance" in the fabrication process requires a coming together of
thought and workmanship. She explains:

> The reification which occurs in writing something down, paint-
> ing an image, modeling a figure, or composing a melody is
> of course related to the thought which preceded it, but what
> actually makes the thought a reality and fabricates things of
> thought is the same workmanship which, through the pri-
> mordial instrument of human hands, builds the other durable
> things of the human artifice. (169)

The writing process, as Arendt suggests, represents a coming together
of cognition and the physical process of making. Thought and workmanship are inevitably bound together; the absence of one signals the
inadequacy of the other. Given Nancy's hopes that her instruction
would extend into students' lives far beyond the classroom and her
sense that the existing model for teaching writing espoused by the
FYWP would not yield this effect, the interrelatedness between her
thought and an available model for workmanship was clearly dis-
rupted. It is here that I find real use, again, in Higgins's contention
that teaching represents a "gray zone" between Arendtian work and
action. For Nancy, the classroom posed a challenge that was dis-
tinctly about mediation and augmentation: Would she acknowledge
her students' potential as writers stunted by poorly selected readings
and grade them generously? Would she emphasize grammatical cor-
rectness in her response to their writing despite the direction she
received in her own training? The extent to which Nancy answered
"yes" to these questions during her first semester challenges us to
think about the fluidity and relationship between action and work,
where teachers' manipulation of the tools and products of the classroom become an act of self-disclosure, a position statement in a
space still considered, by Arendt, safe enough for experimentation.

As Nancy's story illustrates, the politics of inherited models for instruction as well as potential disconnects between teacher and curricula present both a serious threat and an opportunity for crucial resistance and reinvention. In the worst cases, graduate student instructors learn quickly to just perform the required functions in order to move on to their major interests, where the teaching of writing gives way to a kind of mechanized laboring and is robbed of the potential contributions (from interesting teachers like Nancy) of new kinds of thinkers and new models of instruction. Perhaps the teaching practicum would do better to function more as a forum for debate and a laboratory for testing the hypotheses of new teachers. Maybe this kind of welcome engagement is the only way we can encourage new teachers who have something tangible and lasting to contribute to students and our field. Surely, from Arendt we learn that the most stunning gains are won when we walk the most complicated middle line, where graduate student writing teachers are student/teachers, invited to write their stories "in pencil": to manipulate the model, question the images, and redraw the lines of understanding a bit, to cross things out, erase, try again, and ultimately create something new. This kind of engagement is enabled by the safety of a middle space between action and work, and between student and teacher, and may be what makes graduate student teachers stay and contribute to the task of making composition matter.

Nancy's first semester experience became exemplary for her evolving relationship to action and work, from her sensitivity to negative peer pressure to her corresponding augmentation of course materials and teaching philosophy. While the other three study participants seemed perhaps less enthusiastic about their teaching roles, or less confident about the particular challenges of their first semesters, studying Nancy's growth through an Arendtian lens illuminates the development of the other study participants along similar lines. Much of Nancy's struggle occurred privately, something she negotiated for herself, and in the confines of her classroom. This strikes me as especially impressive, given the pressures of the first semester of graduate school and teaching. However, the other study participants each found an opportunity, mediated and supported by the teaching practicum course, to think through some aspect of the "model" for writing instruction that they had originally inherited. After much frustration with the pressure to grade endless student drafts, Anjel and Shirley joined forces and theorized an alternate approach, "interactive grading," which they collaborated on for a final paper for the practicum course. Both also experimented with the practice during the first semester, though such experimentation was preliminary; in their final practicum paper, they proposed integration of their revised grading practice in future classes. Tess, too, used the practicum to explore foundational composition scholarship, asking the kinds of questions perhaps most relevant to her early confusion about how to teach writing. In what follows, I consider these moments in light of the importance, as established in the analysis of Nancy's experiences, of striking a protected middle space between teaching and learning for graduate student teachers. It is in this vein that new graduate student teachers are able to be actors and workers, change agents and also contributors to the tools and products of writing instruction.

WORKING IT OUT: FIGHTING "THE MACHINE" AND THE THREATS OF GRADE CONSUMPTION

Both enrolled in the MA creative writing program, Anjel and Shirley quickly began to work as partners, helping each other with assignments, lesson plans, and schedules. They typically organized the week together so that they were teaching the same lessons around the same time. This collaboration culminated in a final project for the teaching practicum course in which each theorized a model of "interactive grading" to be instituted the following semester. Interactive grading involved a working, collaborative relationship between teacher and student in which a grade was discussed, assessed, and finally agreed upon.[4] Shirley came up with the idea while conferencing with students at a time when she felt particularly frustrated with the grading process. In many ways, this story stands as a resistance to assessment standards and procedures, the paper load for first-year writing instructors, and, especially, students' demand for grades. This pressure can be particularly intense when teachers are new and thus unsure about administrative and student expectations around grading. As discussed in Nancy's experience, these two sets of expectations are often in conflict with each other. In Anjel and Shirley's design of interactive grading, we see a desire (similar to Nancy's) for studenthood, a request to "partner" with their students in an effort to figure something out. This revised position came in response to the pressure to be, instead, a nameless, all-powerful "grading machine."

Attempting to explain the roots of interactive grading during the course of her first semester struggle, Shirley wrote the following history:

> In a period of despair/inspiration, I decided not to grade one set of papers, but to have students grade themselves, in conference. When they came into my office, I handed them their paper, had them read the first paragraph out loud, and then tell me what the paper intended to prove, based on what they read. . . . At the end of each conference, I asked the student what grade they thought the paper should receive. To my surprise, most of them gave themselves the same grade, or lower, than I would have given them. This told me that they were capable of critical thought towards their own work, and of taking responsibility for their own revision. I realized that if I took myself out of the equation, or at least pushed myself to the side, they could reach the goal with minimal assistance. (practicum final paper)

One of the most striking features of this initial experience was that it appeared to reinforce or validate Shirley's own grading standards ("To my surprise, most of them gave themselves the same grade, or lower, than I would have given them"). Shirley's "surprise" here was an admission, in a sense, that she had much to learn about students' relationship to assessment and their own writing. Shirley's "despair" was undoubtedly assuaged by this validation, and some of the grading burden was lightened when she learned that students were "capable" of understanding assessment and "taking responsibility for their own revisions . . . with minimal assistance." Shirley now had permission to take herself "out of the equation," or at least to push herself "to the side." This revelation came in marked contrast to the original conception of the role of "grader," which she discusses in her practicum paper:

> Grading can be the bane of the composition instructor's existence. Even if one subscribes to the empowered education theory, of spreading authority around the classroom and putting the responsibility of learning into the hands of students, the onus is still on the instructor when it comes to grading. . . . They [the students] rely on the instructor to tell them how to "fix" each paper.

Especially for the new teacher, students who "rely on the instructor to tell them how to 'fix' each paper" suggest a degree of responsibility that may exceed the new teacher's sense of preparedness and conviction. This recalls the student revolt staged after Tess doled out many low grades and her subsequent cowering, anxious response. Many new teachers do not feel enough self-confidence to take on the pressures associated with grading, from student disappointment to the articulation of clear assessment criteria. The conversational format of Shirley and Anjel's assessment approach relieved some of this pressure and also attempted to close off the option of simple "fixing," pushing students toward rethinking and process-oriented revision.

Building on these goals, Anjel unknowingly tapped into an age-old composition studies debate: process versus product. It is particularly interesting to observe Anjel's discussion in light of Arendt's contention that, in school, students inherit an "old world" that they ultimately must change. Functioning in his capacity as student in the practicum course, Anjel was able to connect his argument in favor of process back to his first-year writing students' over-focus on grades, suggesting that their concern about grades paralyzed much of their revision process. He wrote:

> I believe that the current grading system in English 50 places too much emphasis on final product. Students worry too much about the grade of each individual paper, and the process of revision becomes less a way of re-seeing and reframing their original argument and more about finding every dangling modifier and

comma splice. Indeed, I have found students loath to change too much in their papers, for fear of getting a worse grade. For many of these freshmen students, grading seems arbitrary and mysterious: feed your paper into the grading machine and it will spit back out a grade. (practicum final paper)

As Anjel perceptively identifies a crucial threat, "grading seems arbitrary and mysterious," we must consider the implications of such mystery on both new teachers and students. The pressure surrounding the grade only intensifies: teachers feel increasingly insecure as students are apt to question and misunderstand their rationale, and students feel less control over how to get the grades they feel they need and deserve. Less control on the students' part may result in their putting added pressure on teachers in the form of demands for the grades they want. Anjel's goal for students was that the revision process be less grade-oriented and grammar driven and more about rethinking and reconceptualizing argument. Certainly, this perspective has its roots in progressive education, in wanting students to take an active role in critical thinking and their own work. Shirley, too, wrote hopefully that "interactive grading will create a student-empowered classroom" (practicum final paper). Beyond idealism, though, Anjel also revealed one side effect of grade-driven students for the writing teacher: "feed your paper into the grading machine and it will spit back out a grade." Surely, the role of "grading machine" feels nondescript, unimportant, and largely anti-intellectual. Just as students might feel as though they do not have a handle on why certain grades happen, new teachers may find themselves unsure of the importance of their own critical thinking abilities and thus swept into an endless, cyclical grading process dangerously reminiscent of Arendtian laboring.[5]

Anjel and Shirley both planned to shift some responsibility away from themselves and onto the students in hopes of creating more of a working partnership between teacher and student. Anjel explained, "By sharing responsibility of grading, I hope that students will take ownership of their own learning. I also believe that interactive grading will reposition myself less as the ultimate classroom authority and more as a partner to their success" (practicum final paper). In this respect, interactive grading also responded to one of Anjel's frustrations with his students' course evaluations: though they enjoyed him as a teacher, they complained that he never gave them the answers, shared his viewpoint, or explained clearly his interpretation of the assigned reading. Instead, Anjel strove to present multiple sides of an issue and to encourage varied and diverse interpretations rather than espouse a more rigid, singular vantage point. He was frustrated that students did not appreciate this approach. Surely, interactive grading also reflected his desire to change students' expectations of the teacher as all-knowing or the "ultimate classroom authority." While Anjel shared Shirley's desire to disrupt her positioning as exclusive grading authority, he was disappointed by students' eventual criticism of his decentered positioning. The evident chasm between Anjel's intentions and students' expectations, as well as his grappling with the tensions between product and process that represent an outdated debate for scholars but appear relevant and important in a new teacher's first semester, signals that we have much to learn about the first semester classroom as a site for understanding disparities between theory and practice in composition. Higgins's formulation of Arendt's position on school as a mediating, safe space where teachers and students must bridge action and work becomes a useful lens for understanding the importance of Anjel and Shirley's efforts.

In his practicum paper, Anjel announced his decision to include interactive grading as a requirement in his next syllabus. Students who did not like the idea would be encouraged to go elsewhere. Despite his commitment to student responsibility and participation, Anjel did not want to engage students in "choosing" the interactive grading approach. Rather, interactive grading would be a requirement of the course so that students could take responsibility for their own work and assessment. I stress this because, beyond a requirement for students, Anjel's move here indicated a reformulation of "who" the teacher would be, as well. In his final paper for the practicum class, Anjel quoted his new syllabus as follows:

We will all be responsible for each other's performance. . . . By sharing the grading responsibility, you will gain a clearer sense of what it takes to edit, proofread, revise, and write on an academic level. If you are uncomfortable with the level of responsibility, I strongly suggest that you withdraw from this section and re-enroll with a different teacher.

Anjel conceptualized interactive grading as a shared, collaborative responsibility. The term "responsibility" is particularly crucial here, as it underscores a mutual commitment to the practices of a distinct classroom space. Students must be on board; if they are not, they are advised to enroll in a different section. Anjel's contention that "we will all be responsible for each other's performance" suggests that, while the teacher is in part responsible for grading, students are equally accountable for the validity of such grades. This move suggests a radical realignment of both teacher and student roles: the teacher will no longer harbor secretive, "mysterious" grading standards and practices, and the student will no longer simply fix mistakes blindly, hoping to hit the correct mystery equation. Notably, the lofty goals for such collaboration echo Arendt's contention that action can happen only in the spirit of "plurality," where the "revelatory quality of action and speech comes to the fore where people are with others and neither for nor against them—that is, in sheer human togetherness" (*Human Condition* 180). Such "togetherness" seems to mirror Nancy's "we're all in this together" identification with her students, where contending with difficult readings involved an "admit it as I work through it" approach. While Anjel did not so openly define his role as "questioning," in fact the collaborative spirit of interactive grading reconfigures the relationship between teacher and student in a way that suggests—in its most idealized version—that the practice of assessment is a shared endeavor, one neither won nor lost but that instead requires honest togetherness in order to be completed effectively.

Before we celebrate the initiation of interactive grading as a distinct, game-changing moment of Arendtian action, Anjel's further discussion of the steps involved remind us that the grading burden still looms large. The size of this challenge is clear in his written description of how he would carry out interactive grading with students:

> I will let him [the student] know where exactly his argument falters, where there are glaring omissions or grammar problems, and where his reading of the text needs to be more fully explained. After going through his paper, I will ask the student to give his paper a grade. After talking about the appropriateness of that grade (if the grade is too high, what needs to be done in further revision; if the grade is too low, what grading criteria is most important), we will assign an agreed upon letter grade to that paper together. After our individual conference, I believe that the student will have a better understanding of what needs to be revised and what I am looking for when grading. (practicum final paper)

According to Anjel, the onus of grading now requires negotiation and argument, which, in one sense, means that the teacher now must publicly explain, defend, and justify his or her grading assessment and suggested revisions in the presence of the student in a face-to-face exchange. Still, that the grade will be "agreed upon" implies that the teacher alone will not stand as sole arbiter of grading standards. Interestingly, Anjel did not give adequate explanation for what might happen when the student staunchly disagrees with the teacher during the discussion of the "appropriateness of that grade." However, most important here is the construction of a kind of system—a model, perhaps—designed to protect against the "grading machine." The effectiveness of this model relies on mediation between teacher and student and a balance between work and action: the negotiation of classroom products, like grades, via Arendt's "sheer human togetherness," which is the very stuff of action. Here again, in an effort to move safely away from the looming threat of laboring along, Anjel and Shirley claimed a middle space, one that invited collaboration with students in a way that belied the role of teacher-as-sole-authority. While Anjel's rhetorical stance describing his role in the interactive grading conference seemed to hold close issues of authority, far more than Nancy's student-identified teaching persona, and to hint at the threat of the endless revisions endured by Tess, I want to insist that the effort of Anjel and Shirley to initiate interactive grading represented an important moment of resistance to an existing order and to the pressure of assuming a role for which they did not feel prepared or eager. The nature of their move exemplifies the blending of action and work, as the moment of invention here is bound permanently to the negotiation and creation of the "record," the grade, that affirms both teacher and student's participation in the class.

Clearly hinted at in Anjel's implementation plan for interactive grading, the race to escape the consumptive, nondescript grading machine comes with serious conceptual challenges. In *The Human Condition*, Arendt expresses her fears that the work of "homo faber"/ the worker, in light of the heightened "demand culture" generated by the increasing use of machines over human hands, stands to degenerate into solely "means end" productivity. She writes, "In place of both utility and beauty, we have come to design products that still fulfill certain 'basic functions' but whose shape will be primarily determined by the operation of the machine" (152). This means that homo faber loses his workmanship, the pride in the created product, as he is swept into the constant rush of public consumption. Anjel pinpointed this increasingly consumptive nature of the first-year composition course when he worried that students revise only to the extent that they can achieve a desired grade, rending the process of revision and the ensuing written product worthless and his role into one of "grading machine."

Anjel painted an image of this all-consuming grading machine from two sides: teacher and student. First-year students' attitude or experience toward grading as "arbitrary and mysterious" is linked to the concept of a "machine," suggesting that our modern-day attitude toward machinery is that it yields our desired result without requiring our understanding or engagement. The machine, in this sense, is likened to magic: put a carrot into a hat and pull out a rabbit. Or, as Anjel described, "feed your paper into the grading machine and it will spit back out a grade." Of course, on the other side of the grading machine is the composition teacher. In truth, the teacher as worker does not have any magic contraption that processes student grades. The work that he or she does, however, is regarded by students as machine-like and thus not something for which students can be equally responsible. Shirley and Anjel's interactive grading innovation was an attempt to resist their status as mechanical and mysterious laborers and thus the spiraling of their grading efforts into Arendtian laboring alone. By requiring students to take part in the grading process, they asked students to meet them in a mediated, collaborative space where roles, grading practices, and assessment standards would be illuminated and augmented. Through this intervention and collaboration, Anjel and Shirley strove to preserve the quality of the grade as a kind of legitimate, valuable classroom artifact while they also sought some refuge from a public role that threatened to consume them.

Shirley and Anjel's attempt to alter their frustrating status as nondescript, mechanical graders and to collaborate with students on assessment unearths Arendt's worries over the future of work, expressed decades earlier in *The Human Condition*. Anjel's concern about students' reluctance to engage in a more complex process of revision resonates with Arendt's fears about a cultural shift in manufacturing: that "which has always been 'a series of steps' has become 'a continuous process,' the process of the conveyor belt and the assembly line" (149). The "process" of conveyor belt and assembly line are, ideally, far distinct from the kinds of processes compositionists speak of when we talk about drafting and revision. Anjel, too, seemed to long for a more idyllic notion of "process" when he wrote that "the process of revision becomes less a way of re-seeing and reframing their original argument and more about finding every dangling modifier and comma splice." The idea of finding these more minor grammatical errors instead of addressing the far messier and more complex conceptual picture fits seamlessly with an urge to keep the conveyor belt moving, to avoid holding up the speed with which one can acquire the grade. Further, it suggests a reluctance to engage with the product, to take the time to alter it on more complicated, intellectual levels. If the desired grade can be achieved without such engagement, and the prospect of creating a durable, lasting product has been largely subsumed by the incessant push for the grade and course credit alone, who can blame the first-year student for hurriedly rushing through the first-year course? Though perhaps first-year composition students are operating more as innocent bystanders than as conspirators in the field's curricular struggles, Arendt suggests that the consequences of the machine's dominance are dismal. With the high-speed productivity of the machine, Arendt notes a dangerous cycle of supply and demand. Production responds to increasing demand in ways that yield a product inconsistent with durability and craftsmanship. The machine's product is only a means to an immediate end; it is not a product designed for long-term human use, nor is it meant to exist as a historical marker in our human fabric. It is, instead, absorbed into the mere process of making, much as the laborer's toils are devoured and rendered useless. Arendt writes, "The question therefore is not whether we are the masters or slaves of our machines, but whether machines still save the world and its things, or if, on the contrary, they and the automatic motion of their processes have begun to rule and even destroy world and things" (*Human Condition* 151). Anjel answers Arendt's question with the contention that the machine has, in fact, "begun to rule and even destroy world and things," at least in the context of the written product in first-year composition. Arendt initially raises the possibility that the machine might not be destructive, that it might "still save the world and its things." In Arendt's hope for the machine, we find language reminiscent of her expectation for action, which, when faced with the inevitable fact that "the lifespan of man running toward death" would "carry everything human to ruin and destruction," serves as the interrupting force that renews the world (246). Here again, then, we find confirmation of Higgins's move to blend action and work, especially as they operate in the mediating space of the classroom. I want to argue that it was particularly when Anjel and Shirley were able to occupy a secure middle space between teacher and student, as facilitated by the practicum paper they had to write, that they were capable of problem solving in light of the grading burden and the kinds of threats to productivity that Arendt most fears. In Anjel and Shirley's design of interactive grading, the craft and skill of both teacher and student writer are not lost to a hyper-focus on the grade itself, nor to an endless and mysterious process of student drafting and teacher feedback. Such design requires a conceptual positioning on the border between action and work.

Because Anjel and Shirley's interactive grading permitted them increased collaboration and, I would argue, identification with students, and because they both used the practicum course as a space in which to work out, in writing, an implementation plan for the following semester, we are reminded of the potential relationship between the purpose of school, for Arendt, and the learning needs of new graduate student writing teachers. In his discussion of the rationale for interactive grading, Anjel grappled with what otherwise seemed like an outdated concern, the balance between process and product in the writing classroom. In light of Arendt's contention that "we destroy everything if we so try to control the new that we, the old, can dictate how it will look," we witness with new eyes Anjel's return to what seems, from the outside, an antiquated discussion (the post-process movement hit its stride in the mid-1990s in composition scholarship). In some ways, resistance to the process movement, posed most vocally by scholars like Gary Olson, Thomas Kent, and Karen Burke LeFevre, parallels Arendt's worries about the overemphasis on process and the ensuing, ineffective "by-product" that results. Olson warns, "Any attempt to construct a generalizable explanation of how something works is misguided in that such narratives inevitably deprivilege the local, even though it is the local where useful 'knowledge' is created" (182). However, process instruction continues to outline the pedagogical approach for new and experienced writing teachers alike, and, interestingly, in his resistance to students' "product" and grade-centered approach to writing, Anjel's description of interactive grading emphasizes the importance of pulling students into the process of drafting, revision, and assessment.

Anjel presents a most compelling paradox in light of Olson's worries, as he at once employed a potentially "generalizing" practice of sending students routinely into the revision process while also exemplifying—in his situatedness as graduate student writing teacher—a kind of "local" point of contact as he negotiated, and attempted to modify, inherited theories and practices. Describing the teacher side of the interactive grading conference, Anjel's focus was all process: "I will let him [the student] know where exactly his argument falters, where there are glaring omissions or grammar problems, and where his reading of the text needs to be more fully explained." It was only when Anjel completed his rounds of attention to process that the focus shifted to product in the form of a grade. At this point, the responsibility also shifted to the student: "After going through his paper, I will ask the student to give his paper a grade." Here, when faced with the necessity of taking a more final, product-centered stance, Anjel eagerly placed the responsibility on the student. After the student has responded, Anjel has to address the grade. However, he would do so from a process stance: "If the grade is too high, what needs to be done in further revision; if the grade is too low, what grading criteria is most important."

A more nuanced view of the post-process movement allows for a kind of coexistence of process strategies, attention to the student text, and engagement with the surrounding social realities that are relevant for writers and their audiences. For Bruce McComiskey, this approach accepts that, while "a piece of writing is 'never finished' . . . most writing is read, is intended to be read, so writers must then be able to account for the ways in which texts are not only produced but also distributed and consumed within specific communities" (42). Anjel's admirable effort to engage student writers in dialogue about grading criteria and revision was an attempt to disrupt his finding that they were "loath to change too much in their papers, for fear of getting a worse grade." At the same time, the fact of grading remains, as does its accompanying criteria; revision is ultimately a response to the unchanging reality that the writing will receive a grade. Engaging students in a collaborative grading process is a kind of standing contradiction if, in fact, the grading criteria are not subject to change based upon the teacher/student collaboration. As Olson claims, application of a process across varied situations (the "local") can be dangerous: ultimately, we may construct a narrative that springs from a process that is not, itself, changeable. This is not collaborative knowledge making but rather the plugging of variables into a set formula. Olson's critique is, of course, about the stasis of the formula.

Despite Anjel's good intentions, his resistance to "grading machine" status faced two unchanging factors not within his control: the grading criteria that were designed by the FYWP, not by Anjel and his students, and the reliance on a revision process that was plugged into these grading criteria. Ultimately, in his effort to avert students' attention from the final product, Anjel inevitably found that he had inherited a teaching practice, process instruction, which existing scholarship had argued to be outdated, and, though he attempted to construct a new model for assessment, he lacked new tools for practice. In other words, Anjel recognized an "old problem" in writing instruction and attempted to "set it right" but inevitably was not prepared "in such a way that a setting-right actually remains possible" (Arendt, *Human Condition* 192). Certainly, within the confines of the practicum, Anjel had a safe space in which to experiment, supported especially by the final paper assignment for the course; however, the safety of this space was in marked contrast to his concurrent role as teacher/grader to his first-year students. Because Anjel seemed to stop just short of aligning with his students in the spirit of Nancy's "admit it as I work through it" approach to teaching, he inevitably and unknowingly uncovered complex theoretical and practical tensions for our field. Many graduate student and adjunct writing teachers feel overwhelmed by the grading burden and students' focus on the grade, but any efforts to disrupt the situation are overshadowed by their potential dislocation from evaluation criteria and theorized approaches to writing instruction. As theoretical trends fall in and out of fashion, the problems of practice remain. The message, if we read through Arendt, is that we are doomed if we fail to give our "world" over with greater cognizance to the "new," whose task it is to remake it. Anjel's example indicates a failure, on the part of composition scholarship, to see the "new" in the newest teachers of first-year writing, the graduate student teachers who staff many classrooms semester after semester.

Given the complex theoretical and practical tensions at work here, how might we make sense of Anjel and Shirley's resistance to the grading machine given our hopes, as a field, of improving the preparation of graduate students to teach writing? While they had no idea their resistance to the grading burden would tap into theoretical debates that stretch the length of composition studies and beyond, their frustration as cogs in a proverbial wheel and effort to make change raise important considerations about the role(s) we assign graduate students in their first semester of teaching. Anjel and Shirley seemed prepared to function as students of writing instruction, to offer their unique take on the world of first-year writing they suddenly inherited, and the practicum course was surely a mediating space that could support such exploration. However, in concurrently assigning them a fixed model for their work—in the form of an assigned syllabus, grading pressures, and a limited, predetermined instructional approach—Anjel and Shirley's efforts at augmentation hit a roadblock given our field's disconnect between theory and practice, between those who theorize the field and those who do most of the classroom teaching.

Most important in the analysis of Anjel and Shirley's attempt at revising an existing model is that it underscored their need, as graduate students, for a supportive atmosphere in which to figure things out. While they attempted to use the practicum course for this purpose, the great contradiction is that their work there did not extend into the concurrent "reality" of the first-year writing classroom in which they occupied the status of teacher. Accordingly, we might think of the former as the more comfortable, more appropriate space for Anjel and Shirley during their first semester as graduate students: it is where they felt most at home trying on various pedagogical approaches and position statements. Only Nancy seemed to transition this mind-set into her first-year classroom, defining a teaching approach on the grounds of her own studenthood. But the potential chasm between the first-year classroom and the practicum course for the other three study participants is an important one. In their work for the practicum, we witness how they might otherwise strategize their own means of keeping afloat, of resisting the otherwise consuming current of laboring alone.

WORKING IT OUT: TESS RE-AUTHORIZES THE MODEL

Tess opens this chapter as an example of the ill effects of premature action on a new graduate student writing teacher. I want to return to her here to consider an alternate experience that perhaps gives us more hope while still reinforcing the often-vulnerable positioning of new graduate student teachers. In her own work for the teaching practicum course, Tess demonstrated a paradox similar to that at the heart of Anjel and Shirley's efforts around interactive grading. Though the first-year writing classroom occasioned a far too glaring, premature public exposure during her first semester, which caused her to embrace a laboring model of instruction—endless drafts and endless revisions—she also attempted to use the practicum class as an opportunity to explore and question inherited models of composition pedagogy. Her peers' efforts demonstrated that such exploration must rely on a blending of Arendtian action and work, which the practicum course is well positioned to facilitate. The remaining challenge is to determine how we can best support new writing teachers in their fraught efforts to transfer this critical exploration and augmentation of foundational composition theory, as students, into an applicable, distinct classroom practice, as teachers.

Arendt's explanation of work as dependent upon "an image beheld by the eye of the mind or a blueprint in which the image already found tentative materialization through work" becomes a source of significant tension in light of Tess's struggle for an instructional model (*Human Condition* 40). As we remember from chapter 2, Tess admitted early on, when faced with her first load of student papers, that she didn't "know how to teach writing" (email, 15 Sept.). At this juncture, the practicum class became, potentially, a mediating space and source of a "blueprint" for instruction. Under the heading "How Do We Teach Revision?," the professor assigned as readings Nancy Sommers's article "Revision Strategies of Student Writers and Experienced Adult Writers" as well as Sondra Perl's essay "The Composing Process of Unskilled Writers at the College Level." Students were then assigned the task of writing a two-page summary of one of them. Tess chose to write on Sommers; her piece is dated exactly one week after I received her frustrated email that first detailed her confusion about teaching writing. In her struggle with Sommers's discussion, Tess illuminated her skills as a student of composition theory, showcasing her ability to understand, as well as her desire to augment, foundational scholarship for classroom application. For Tess, however, the task of actually augmenting her inherited model for instruction remained out her reach, at least in terms of a transferable pedagogical practice for use in her current first-year writing classroom. It is here that the role of the practicum as a mediating space for such negotiation and implementation stands to most fully exemplify Higgins's goals for Arendtian action and work in the classroom.

In her practicum paper, Tess decently summarized Sommers's work but then returned to her questions about how to teach writing and revision without much added insight. Tess explained Sommers's position in a way that defined revision in abstract terms and thus fell short of her own interest in understanding how to enact it in a classroom. She wrote: "Sommers details the components of revision: the recognition of dissonance (incongruities in meaning between what is said and what is written) and the rearrangement and adding that bring new meaning. Writing and revision are defined by a process" (practicum review paper). While Tess understood Sommers's point that unskilled writers tend to revise on the level of word choice rather than engage in a larger conceptual re-seeing of their written product, she had doubts about whether students would be able to move beyond this stumbling point. She explained her concern:

> If I am asking them to develop their argument, to bring in quotes and examples from the text, they should be adding ideas to their papers, rather than crossing out and putting in different words. Since I am having them look at their papers as an experienced writer would regarding the "form and shape of their argument" . . . will they be able to do this, even after taking a few days to discuss what argument is?

Tess made clear that she understood Sommers's distinction between students' tendency toward unskilled revision strategies and the more ideal, more abstract strategies employed by experienced writers.

However, Sommers's article had not answered her questions about the first-year college students in her class. Namely, Tess wondered, "Will they be able to do this?"

Tess's doubt about her students' abilities pointed to larger insecurities about her ability to apply Sommers's more sophisticated conception of revision in her classroom. In the following longer quotation, she struggled with her own questions in the final paragraph of her written response to Sommers:

> Now that I know I must teach revision, and that I must teach it as a process rather than as an exclusive step between first draft and final draft, how do I teach it? Part of teaching it is to liberate them from the rules that confine them to "word or sentence level" corrections. They need "strategies for handling the whole essay." . . . Does the instruction of revision involve using a paper discussion week to say, "This is the process of revision . . ."? You will understand that writing is not a linear activity, and revision is not one point on that line. Writing is a process that contains within it the process of revision, which you are constantly doing as you write. Or, rather, is teaching revision embedded in the activities and peer work in which students take part during paper discussion weeks? (practicum review paper)

Despite the information provided by the practicum in the form of well-known theoretical pieces by Sommers and Perl, Tess struggled with the same "how to" questions that she had only a week earlier. Her greatest confusion revealed itself in a distinction between a more conceptual explanation and more practical, hands-on, activity-driven instruction. Specifically, she tried to clarify whether "teaching" revision is about directive instruction—"This is the process of revision" and "You will understand"—or experiential instruction, such as "activities and peer work." While Tess did not seem to get an answer from Sommers on this question, she ended her essay with the sweeping declaration, "By training students to look at their classmates' writing, they obtain the skills necessary to look at their writing with new eyes; they get a sense of seeing the larger issues at play in their composition." This sentence seems to gloss over Tess's questions about "how" to "train" students to complete such tasks, as it comes immediately after the above-quoted struggle over teaching strategies. The ending of Tess's piece reads as if she was trying not to exceed the specified page limit for the assignment and simply attempted to wrap up her own questions with a "fix all" motion. In reality, "training students to look at their classmates' writing" is bogged down by Tess's questions about exactly what successful student writing should look like and how to talk about it.

Tess's wrangling with foundational scholarship and her search for a method of instruction underscore the significance of what new teachers do with inherited models or blueprints for their work. On a basic level, the "products" of the first-year writing classroom include students' completion of course requirements, especially their written work, and the earning of grades assigned by the teacher. On a more sophisticated level, the classroom product for the new teacher is the creation of a method of instruction, a way of talking about and teaching writing that is presented to students as his or her craft. Tess's frustrations about what and how to teach writing outline the holes in her blueprint and the ensuing challenges to her role as worker. Because Tess's struggle is not highly unusual or surprising, we need to assess the significance of a more widespread breakdown between what new teachers are doing in the classroom and the image "beheld by the eye of the mind" of our field, if such an image securely exists. Further, though, if we apply Arendt's model for schooling as a moderately protective space in which the "young" are given what has become the "old" world with the hope that they will learn how to radicalize it and make it new, we must look at Tess's engagement with Sommers as a ripe moment that fell short of its potential.

If she is to realize her potential for contributing to the existing "world" of how to teach writing, Tess must think of herself, first, as a student of composition pedagogy, someone who must absorb the existing "stuff" of the field (from the composition course itself and all its components, including assignments, reading materials, and student writing, to the overarching models for instruction in the form of foundational scholarship). However, in this process, to return to Higgins, she must also be invited to experiment, to operate as both actor and worker, to manipulate the model and allow it to unfold an evolving, changing document. While this formulation is reminiscent of her own vision for school, Arendt seems to disallow the worker such license when she argues in *The Human Condition* that the worker's model is unchanging: "The image or model whose shape guides the fabrication process not only precedes it, but does not disappear with the finished product, which it survives intact, present, as it were, to lend itself to an infinite continuation of fabrication" (141). While Tess seemed able to understand Sommers conceptually, she appeared to resign herself, by the close of her response paper, to the failure of translation because she was not able to manipulate Sommers's model toward her own needs.[6]

But why was Tess unable to manipulate the model? Did she have the sense that the model descends from an authority—the FYWP? foundational scholarship? the "field"?—with which she was simply not authorized to reckon? Although Tess struggled to translate Sommers's work into a practice, we cannot assume that, first of all, any practical model (either directive or more constructive, experiential instruction) would necessarily match what Sommers herself might deem appropriate. Second, when new teachers implement a model for practice, unexpected outcomes often cast them back to rework or revise the model. This was true of the experiences of the other study participants, as well. Thus, I am inclined to agree with Higgins in his contention that Arendt herself had a more flexible sense of the codependency between action and work and that her more stringent definitions belie the complexity of her own thinking. I want to point, once again, to Arendt's valuing of the US Constitution, that written tome and model for a government, as an example of action due to its status as a continuously evolving document (Higgins 437). In Tess's grappling with Sommers's language, we find a similar potential for the renewal of an existent document. School is the space most capable, if we follow Higgins's argument, of facilitating such renewal, given it offers some safety for experimentation and also bridges the goals of action and work. Higgins writes of the trying on of masks so appropriate to school's mediated and ideally safe space: "We search for words we can make our own. We search for the phrase that will not ring hollow, that taps into something authentic in us, that we can speak with conviction. So it is not that we exist simply as ourselves and subsequently adopt roles and disguises. . . . We search for those roles that finally put us in touch with who we are" (433). In this apt description, we can hear Tess's engagement with Sommers in a new way, one that suggests a rooting around in Sommers's words for those that best fit her current situation. That she did not find complete and instant connection perhaps only points to the importance that she augment the model to better suit her needs. In Tess, especially, we see the consequences of these missed connections, and, in reflection, the mission of the practicum is newly delineated.

As we learn most vividly in Tess's case, not only must new teachers struggle with existing models for instruction, but these struggles are often dangerously, prematurely exposed and public. In addition to the public sphere occupied by actors, Arendt allows for a public space for workers, too: "His public realm is the exchange market, where he can show the products of his hand and receive the esteem which is due him" (*Human Condition* 160). This public, too, we learn through Tess, comes with the threat of overexposure and leads, just as with the premature push into action, into absorption into laboring. The public space afforded Tess was a contentious one where neither teacher nor students were confident about "the products of his hand." Arendt writes quite assuredly of "esteem," but when we think about new teachers—and especially Tess's first semester— the idea of esteem as an embedded part of the exchange becomes fraught with oversimplification. In Tess's first semester, none of the participants in the production process—teacher or students—were confident about their work or, for that matter, held each other, as workers, in particularly high regard.

Tess's insecurities about her students' perception of her as a teacher only increased as the semester wore on. In part, I want to attribute this growing insecurity to her unfortunate experience of premature public exposure and a failed opportunity to augment her inherited models of instruction in the security of a more mediated space that privileged her role as "student." Toward the end of her first semester,

Tess described her own anxiety to me in an email: "I am nervous about student evaluations. I am so afraid that my students are going to say that I totally sucked, and I didn't know what I was talking about, and I was confusing. . . . Because we kept getting fed information as we went along, I constantly had to backtrack, and I feel like this hurt my credibility with the students" (17 Nov.). Perhaps Tess's nerves in part contributed to her apparent blaming of the FYWP for hurting her public credibility. However, her language here speaks to the tentative formation of a model for instruction ("Because we kept getting fed information as we went along, I constantly had to backtrack"), as well as to a sense that credibility rests in an unchanging model. In other words, for Tess, a more credible teacher does not present her pedagogy as experimental or influx. For this reason, Tess was unable to adapt a pedagogy similar to Nancy's "admit it as I work through it" student-identified approach, which allowed her to extend Arendt's ideas about school and studenthood into her first teaching experience. Of course, Anjel and Shirley's augmentation of their inherited assessment model ran into a fate similar to Tess's.

WORKING AHEAD

My analysis here is not meant to suggest a kind of "dead end" for new graduate student writing teachers, and certainly I want to underscore the potential inherent in all of the study participants' efforts to revise the model, not to celebrate only Nancy's more complete transfer of her learning efforts to her first classroom. The challenge, in part, is to rethink how we construct new writing teachers' first "publics." Arendt has been criticized for a tendency to valorize an elite "public sphere," one built on competitive exclusion rather than inclusiveness.[7] While resistance to these critiques has been amply argued, in fact in Arendt's worker's exchange market, as well as in the actor's even more dynamic arena of politics, there is an expectation of excellence that seems to disallow error and revision, even with Arendt's caveats about forgiveness considered. But Arendt's thought is anything but easily categorized, as I think Higgins's reformulation of action and work for the classroom usefully demonstrates. Accordingly, we return to Arendt and our new graduate student writing teachers with another set of questions: In what ways can we value the perhaps shakily conceived work of the new teacher as an augmentation of existing, inherited models? To what extent do we conceive of foundational scholarship in composition as potentially "old" and in need of innovation and interruption? How might the practicum course serve as a mediating space between graduate students' double role as student/teacher, inviting experimentation and the transfer of their new adaptations, sketched in pencil, perhaps, into the real space of their first writing classrooms?

Rethinking our construction of new teachers' publics, then, involves extending Arendt's conception of schooling beyond the practicum course into their first classrooms, somehow allowing them to operate, always, as student/teachers, much as Nancy demonstrated. In so doing, we might be able to more fully witness their grappling with what has become—perhaps even without our knowledge— "old" in the field while, as a field, we seek ways to support and celebrate this grappling and augmentation. Drawing on Arendt's metaphor of a table as representative of the shared public space necessary for action, Higgins explains well the potential richness of this configuration:

> The table is a nice metaphor for public space, the space where we find ourselves suddenly separated by something we have in common, something that by its very commonality draws us together from different directions. It is because we sit at the same table, that we sit on different sides of it. It is because we are sitting across from someone that we suddenly realize our own angle on the matter. (418)

While all the study participants embodied Arendt's hopes for action in their spirit of interruption and invention with regard to existing practices and theories, Tess, Shirley, and Anjel seemed to need greater support and enhanced resources in order to get their ideas functional in the real space of the writing classroom. Thus, their stories exist as a fascinating paradox, where we can see not only the crosscurrents between theory and practice but also the conflicting roles of being, for the first time and all at once, a student and teacher of writing.

While Nancy seemed more willing to disregard the authoritative models of instruction and assessment she inherited, I believe the other three study participants were perhaps more fully representative of graduate students new to teaching. They were simultaneously capable, interested, and insightful but also bound up and contained by the pressures of a system not of their own design. Higgins's project in his reformulation of Arendt's notion of schooling asks us to nurture students' and teachers' collective potential for making change by giving them a space for experimentation and by cultivating a natural codependency between Arendtian work and action—allowing for a continuously evolving "document" of pedagogical practice and assessment, for example—that makes change likely and possible.

Perhaps this is yet another call for more of a collaborative, workshop environment for the practicum. Not only should new teachers be invited to engage the materials of composition theory and pedagogy in the practicum setting, but perhaps they should also have the opportunity to sketch and try out alternate approaches. I do not believe that this kind of engagement should necessarily be required—there will always be new teachers who want to teach the syllabus exactly or who agree whole-heartedly with each piece of scholarship they read—and surely requirement would defeat the purpose anyway. This is, instead, about nurturing thinking and highly skilled writing teachers. When we fall short of this task, maybe we are creating machines; for sure, we are undermining composition as a discipline and the work of the writing teacher as a craft.

I should add that it is easy to make sweeping practical suggestions that fail to transfer realistically from one local context to another. I have tried to avoid that here, and surely numerous discussions of model programs are available for WPAs searching for ideas that fit. Instead, my goal has been to offer a lens for inquiry, a way of examining programs and new teachers' experiences across a broad spectrum. Thinking through Arendt allows us to ask questions about what action and work look like at widely different institutions and about how models for instruction are generated and to explore the myriad ways in which we might occasion opportunities to safeguard our newest writing teachers against the threat of labor alone. Perhaps, if we think through Arendt, we may find ways to avoid losing the valuable products of writing teachers' efforts while encouraging their continued invention and manipulation of existing models. When we fail to pause, study, question, and think about what we ask new teachers to do in the classroom, we are inevitably allowing their efforts to be swept away like labor's harvest. They learn dangerous lessons from this experience: most crucially, they learn that the pedagogical efforts of the writing teacher do not make for serious work.

4

Thinking What We Are Doing:
Knowledge Making in the Trenches

THIS BOOK MARKS AN EFFORT to think about the preparation and support of graduate students as they become teachers of first-year writing. I have not described a model program or offered a set of best practices, as I believe such would be a potential misuse of theory as dislocated from diverse contexts. Instead, I have explored how Hannah Arendt's theoretical model functions as a way of reading a set of local experiences. I would like to see how others might apply these concepts to still other contexts, and I anticipate varied results. Ultimately, my sense is that Arendt's theoretical model invites us to think critically and deeply about our field's use of new graduate student teachers, how we prepare them for the classroom, and to what extent these early pedagogical experiences might affect how writing is taught, researched, and theorized more broadly.

Arendt worries in *The Human Condition* about imbalance in her theoretical model and especially about the threat that labor will overtake all we do. This threat looms constantly, of course, in part because the concepts are inherently dependent upon each other. From the opening of the book, she makes a plea for "a reconsideration of the human condition from the vantage point of our newest experiences and our most recent fears" (5). Arendt's concern is that any less will result in "the heedless recklessness or hopeless confusion or complacent repetition of 'truths' which have become trivial and empty," which are "among the outstanding characteristics of our time" (5). Arendt's solution to such dangerous complacency is deceptively simple: "It is nothing more than to think what we are doing" (5). In the world of first-year composition, the task of "thinking what we are doing" is far more monumental than it seems. Staffing issues, a divide between theory and practice (particularly because those doing the theory and those doing most of the teaching can be quite separate), and the overwhelming number of undergraduate students who need to meet the first-year writing requirement make critical reflection crucial but also sometimes secondary to daily concerns.

Still, Arendt's concern over the "complacent repetition of 'truths' which have become trivial and empty" is worthy of pause amid daily challenges. What are the "truths" of our time in composition theory and teaching? And further, have they become somewhat "trivial and empty"? Are we guilty of "complacent repetition"? I do fear that certain aspects of the preparation and support of new graduate students to teach writing have become easily accepted truths that, troublesome though they may be, are losing their urgency as the prospect of "fixing them" remains difficult. In part, WPAs who wrestle heroically with the very real problem of exploited labor in composition face the added problem of accounting for the split in their workforce between graduate students and contingent faculty, a diversity that easily devolves into a kind of "melting pot" of exploited laborers. Marc Bousquet acknowledges as much in the collection *Tenured Bosses and Disposable Teachers: Writing Instruction in the Managed University* when discussing the availability of published advice for adjuncts: "This kind of discourse frequently is permitted to pass as the voice of composition labor—commonly to the exclusion or marginalization of the very different voice represented, for example, by the fifty-campus movement of organized graduate employees" (19). Still, this acknowledgment hardly addresses the very complex challenge faced by WPAs who must prepare, support, and oversee a staff consisting of primarily two "sets" of teachers with very different orientations to the university and their roles in it. Accordingly, I want to argue that graduate student writing teachers' needs are particular to their very positioning, their unique moment in time, which is defined largely by their intention to join what they see as the professoriate: that narrow sliver of tenured, full-time faculty who publish scholarship and, interestingly, do not teach much first-year writing.

The challenges at Public U are honest ones, and the faculty, staff, and administrators at that university are hardworking, informed, and well intentioned. While I reject using theory as a generalizing tool, I also reject the notion that one local context can be universally representative. However, the challenges faced at Public U are neither new nor unique. The accounts of graduate students in this book are not meant to serve as an indictment of Public U as an isolated place. Rather, this book offers one angle on the admittedly complex and ongoing institution that is composition in the university. Fifteen years ago, Susan Miller complained of composition's "illegitimacy," a status secured by its "version of historical legitimacy in rhetoric and its limited self definition as a freshman course," which has allowed "all departments devoted to the 'best' written language to perpetuate the claim that they can judge, and dismiss, the majority's perpetually worst" (76). I sit here, years later, writing about this very "freshman enterprise"; obviously, we have not managed to leave it alone (and perhaps for good reason). This notion of "limited self definition" seems to extend to issues of prepackaged syllabi, course readings, and assignments, which introduce graduate students to a more fixed, mechanistic course than a discipline that requires their curricular inventions. But it also seems to extend to graduate students themselves, especially the degree to which they define themselves against, or as distanced from, this very enterprise. In graduate students—their aspirations, their perceptions, their very newness—we see the tensions and complexities of our field cracked open in a particularly vulnerable way.

In pointing to this vulnerability, I do not want to suggest that much progress hasn't been made or that new innovations are not happening each day in the preparation of new graduate students to teach writing. However, I also want to argue that the very complicated positioning of WPAs—the acknowledged, and often conflicted, "managers" of first-year writing—only adds to the difficulty of getting at the specificity of graduate students' needs and also what it is they have to offer our field. This complicated positioning is plagued by tensions over what "counts" as scholarship in the university. In "Not Even Joint Custody: Notes from an Ex-WPA," Douglas Hesse offers an honest portrayal of his own navigation of this murky administrator/scholar line:

One price has been my disappointing realization that I'll be one of the few chairs of CCCC not to have published a single-authored book by the time I begin office. My writing energies were channeled in other ways, arguably doing some professional good. For example, I note that as of last week, I've put 821 messages on the WPA listserv since 1995. (505)

Hesse's acknowledgment here raises questions about what research and publication might look like in the context of first-year writing administration. Like Hesse, Nancy Sommers describes her complicated location between administration and more traditional notions of scholarship:

I have been evaluated more on my administrative skills as a cruise director and actuary, even a sheriff, than as a writer. The college gives me the responsibility for the writing instruction of 1,650 students each year but never asks, "What do you write?" As an academic I would be invisible if I had not chosen or stumbled into my role as researcher. (514)

Sommers is saved, made "visible," by the role most recognizable to the traditional university. As researcher, she is what the university values and occupies a role with which it most fully identifies.

But the distinction Sommers makes here points to important considerations about how knowledge making happens in the specific context of composition in the university, given the many tensions that swirl around it. In his essay "Knowledge Work, Teaching Work, and Doing Composition," Christopher Ferry lays bare common anxieties among compositionists about our specific brand of knowledge making:

We read student texts, not "great" texts. We do not write groundbreaking analyses or exegeses but rather responses to these modest efforts. This is what disturbs us most, that compositionists might not be, as Kurt Spellmeyer says, "knowledge-workers" . . . , trading in big ideas but instead teamsters, performing the heavy lifting necessary to keep the university afloat. (249)

Interestingly, this self-conscious identification with inferior texts—and I remain unsure about the extent to which it is representative of our collective psyche—presents some contrast to notions of knowledge making in the broader university. According to Ferry, "academic professionals . . . must preserve the class system so as not to reveal the nature of their own work, which is not teaching but instead knowledge-making" (247). Thus, "work" in composition exists on a fault line between "current institutional norms" and all the rest of what we do, which is, most notably, teaching (247). Ferry's project, ultimately, is to argue—as have others—"for the dignity of knowledge work and teaching work, to show that they are inextricably bound" (243). However, in his admission of inferiority—"we read student texts, not 'great' texts"—Ferry also points earnestly to the embedded difficulty of doing scholarship in composition while operating, simultaneously, as a member of the larger university culture.

I want to argue here that, for WPAs, these tensions lurk when they face each cohort of new writing instructors—again, that disjointed cadre of graduate students and contingent faculty—and the fact of these complex layers is an inseparable part of the story of this field. In "Practica, Symposia, and Other Coercive Acts in Composition Studies," Bonnie Kyburz offers a window into the limitations of her role as "teacher" and "writing program administrator," given her complicated and often conflicted positioning:

> I am talking here about leadership, a loathsome term we associate with corporate culture, a precision-oriented term that wants to disambiguate the real experience of working together with variously prepared teachers towards a massively difficult task that presumably requires the delineating action of a "mission statement" or set of desired "outcomes." (67)

Kyburz describes the label "leader" as a burden assigned by a larger, more corporate university culture on behalf of which the WPA reluctantly functions as a kind of arm. Kyburz is self-consciously aware that the "variously prepared teachers" under her leadership may equally disdain the corporate connotations of the term. Ultimately, she proposes that those teaching the practicum course spend more time listening—even "hearing" silent resistance—to the concerns, proposals, questions, and protestations of the newest teachers. Echoing Kyburz's personal admission, we can see that each of the graduate students in this study struggled with—and against—the leadership positions they inherited. These struggles revealed at least a peripheral awareness of the tensions that ensnarl composition in the larger university. Nancy, in particular, seemed most astute when she rallied against the idea that "academics could dismiss all the other people in the world" by caring only about scholarship over—or as distinct from—teaching. She went on to insist that "half the time I think I should just become a high school teacher because . . . I want to teach and I want normal people to be able to appreciate writing and literature" (exit interview). Nancy's musing here revealed her identification of her first-year writing classroom as only about teaching and not, at all, about scholarship, not representative of what academics do. In other words, as a new graduate student, she learned—perhaps accidentally—that the composition classroom was not a rich site for knowledge production, the kind valued in the larger university.

Given Ferry's discussion—which draws on like-minded voices, including Bruce Horner, Jerry Herron, and others—we know that Nancy was not entirely wrong in her assumption about the problematic line between teaching and scholarship. "Knowledge making" in composition still struggles to be what it often is: a studious amalgamation of teaching practice, classroom experiences, and student texts, as well as more "traditional" theory and scholarship. However, Nancy left the potential for knowledge making borne of the composition classroom entirely out of the equation: either one teaches composition, or one becomes an academic and dismisses "all the other people in the world" who do not "do" scholarship. In other words, at the end of her first semester, Nancy did not demonstrate a broader awareness of the kind of intellectual work that Ferry, and so many others, argue for and for which WPAs are best positioned to do (and which they are doing, all the time).

Nancy's innocent ignorance, set against the backdrop of the very real tensions around what "counts" as scholarship in the university, as well as the honest and often conflicted positioning of WPAs—like

Kyburz—charged with the task of preparing graduate student teachers, unveil a crucial communication gap. Any hope for a bridge—between teaching and knowledge making, between graduate student writing teachers and WPAs, between first-year writing and the larger university—necessitates a return to Arendt's notion of school. We remember Arendt's contention, in "The Crisis in Education," that those charged to educate the "young" to fix our world, ever out of joint, stand as "representatives of a world for which they must assume responsibility although they themselves did not make it, and even though they may, secretly or openly, wish it were other than it is" (189). When we think about the task of presenting this "world" of composition in the university to a new group of graduate student writing teachers, we must contend with our relationship to all that defines composition and its positioning in the university today. The preparation of graduate students to teach writing needs to be continuously immersed in what we know about our writing programs, our undergraduate students, the ways in which writing pedagogy has been researched and theorized, and—I would argue—this still murky story of first-year writing's conflicted relationship to the larger university, to the existence of WPAs, and to what it means to make "knowledge" in this field. When we can prepare new writing teachers with an honest consideration of "what we are doing," we are—according to Arendt—equipping them to one day join this world, more fully, as change makers. Our frequent failure to give graduate students the full picture has made the loss of graduate students to other fields and other interests our own disciplinary failure. This failure, I would argue, comes not from ill intent but perhaps as an acknowledgment that it is difficult to determine what to present of our world, "out of joint" as it is, to these eager (or sometimes less-than-eager) newcomers. The truth is that there is real work going on in writing programs throughout, across, and in the university, and particularly in the first-year program where writing plants its roots. But this exciting work happens amid the swirling sea that defines the still-conflicted positioning of composition in the university.

If we follow Nancy's lead, and perhaps her peers' longing, and grant our graduate student teachers permission to be students even as they are teachers, we invite them into a more sheltered space in which they can figure out their own relationship to the fraught task of knowledge making in composition. But what might this student/ teacher construction look like in practice? There are, increasingly, fine and diverse examples of the ways in which we can invite graduate students more fully into this fold.[1] Sally Barr Ebest's book *Changing the Way We Teach: Writing and Resistance in the Training of Teaching Assistants* presents one compelling effort to pull graduate students more deeply into their own learning. Ebest argues that, partly, at the heart of graduate students' common resistance to their teacher training experience rests the fact that practicum faculty seldom model the kind of intensive, student-centered writing pedagogy they want the graduate student teachers to learn and employ (132). The goal of the practicum, then, for Ebest, is that we "help our graduate students reformulate their schema regarding teaching and learning" (118). Ebest proposes the incorporation of action research into this effort, inviting graduate students to conduct their own explorations into the needs of their first-year writing students, thereby becoming knowledge makers even as they are learning to teach. I applaud this effort but also must point to the missing piece, in light of our taking full responsibility for the world into which we initiate these new graduate students, which rests in the overarching conflicts that define composition and its positioning in terms of its role in the larger university. Accordingly, graduate students might wrestle with questions such as: What does it mean to implement a teaching approach, a "schema"—like process pedagogy—in a field that has already theorized its demise? In what ways does the conflicted notion of leadership—to the extent that graduate students as teachers share, with Kyburz, a kind of inherited, but often alienated, position of authority as university representative—inform the ways in which assessment is enacted in the classroom?

My questions here are musings meant to make room for more context-specific investigations. However, at root, the potential of this kind of initiation into not only the first-year writing classroom but also composition as a field rests in defining teacher preparation in terms of a middle space between teaching and learning, where graduate students are allowed to hitch their teaching approach to the very fact of their studenthood. This, it seems, becomes essential if we are to safeguard graduate students' early teaching experiences against devolution into Arendtian laboring alone. In the middle space, where the practicum course, WPAs, and perhaps more advanced graduate student teaching mentors offer these newest teachers the necessarily malleable and quickly-becoming-out-of-date world of composition, they are at once protected and encouraged to experiment.[2] In so doing, graduate student teachers, too, embody the middle space in their approach to teaching writing: augmenting received materials and information, mediating, for their own students, the world as it is with hopes of future change. With such effort, graduate students also operate in what Christopher Higgins calls the "gray zone" between action and work, initiating change through the revision of the durable "stuff" of the field: teaching philosophies, curricula, assignments, research, and scholarship.

The dangers, for new graduate student writing teachers, of existing anywhere other than in this gray zone, in the form of a premature public exposure and nonnegotiable directives about what and how to teach, are anticipated in Arendt's worries about society's potential absorption in laboring alone.[3] She writes that this "laboring society" will be marked by the "non"-individual whose "only active decision . . . [will be] to let go, so to speak, to abandon his individuality, the still individually sensed pain of living, and acquiesce in a dazed, tranquilized, functional type of behavior" (*Human Condition* 23). While this image is a jarring one, and surely would make for a boring class (for all involved), the dangers of excessive laboring in the writing classroom matter, particularly to the extent that such may silence graduate students' other potentialities. Still, this is not to suggest that there does not exist a "laboring stage" to new teachers' first classroom experience, and surely it may be rich and formative in its own right. This is the stage during which new teachers spend countless hours each night on lesson plans, are stuck in endless piles of papers that need grades, and often retrace their steps as students sit before them, staring on. What matters, though, is not that we eradicate this stage from new teachers' experience—I don't think we should, or that we could—but that we respond to it in ways that do not allow laboring to become all they do and invite, instead, graduate students' eventual contributions to research, program revisions, and curricular developments.

The sense that one is constantly making an effort that doesn't "stick" but instead is perpetually wiped away can be draining and pull a new graduate student dangerously away from his or her identification with teaching and with the discipline of composition—first-year classroom included—as a space for knowledge making. It is at this critical juncture where, as Nancy seemed to perceive so clearly, teaching happens in the first-year writing classroom and scholarship happens as you leave this teaching behind. As Tess was increasingly consumed by labor in her first semester, she felt her grasp of academics slipping: "I am trying to write this 505 [required literary theory course for all new PhD students at Public] paper—and was sick all day long—because the 9:40 class just kept popping up in my mind" (email, 20 Sept.). A major problem here, particularly when thinking about a graduate student who came to school to study something other than composition and/or rhetoric, is that she suddenly faced a choice: her studies or her teaching. Teaching was not part of her graduate education, not a potential locale for future intellectual work or success as a graduate student. Though Nancy detested that some of her peers chose their studies, while she felt a stronger identification with the classroom, she perceived the options—the either/or—just as clearly as Tess. And that is cause for far greater concern than the presence of an openly struggling new teacher who is treading water while calling out for rescue.

In its purest form, Arendtian action represents this heroic "rescue," the "miracle that saves the world" (*Human Condition* 247). Both the effects and impetus for action are "faith and hope," which Arendt often refers to in *The Human Condition* as "love of the world" (247). In other words, we initiate change because we believe in our common project—the "world" for Arendt—and in the potential of our actions to matter. Toward the end of *The Human Condition*, Arendt links this notion of action—which she also calls "natality"—to its earliest biblical metaphor: "It is faith and hope for the world that found perhaps its most glorious and most succinct expression in the few words with which the Gospels announced their 'glad tidings': 'A child has been born unto us'" (247). While continuing to reject the notion of graduate students as the children Arendt seems most intent on protecting, I want to suggest that the task posed to those responsible for initiating graduate students into composition as a field—teaching and scholarship bound together—is to search for ways to preserve their potential "love" for this world. As Arendt suggests, the key here is that we somehow also protect them from this world, at least partially, by not pushing them too soon into the pressures of self-identity and public stances, so that they have the space in which to figure that all out. But, as anyone knows who has ever loved another honestly, Arendt also insists that we owe the "young" full disclosure, mediated and augmented though it may be, about what this world of ours looks like so far. Only when equipped with the security of a forgiving, more flexible space for experimentation and the whole story about composition's conflicted roots in higher education do graduate students have any chance of real connection and real change agency.

Action, then, is a far cry from individualism or personal identity and more about a collective investment in making the world "new" over and over again for each other, which is why Arendt insists on action's dependency on "plurality" or human togetherness (*Human Condition* 176). I would argue that graduate students seldom identify as part of this collective in the first-year writing context, which explains not only their likely perception that they must choose between being a teacher and being a scholar but also the long-standing reputation of the practicum course as a conflicted space that serves neither option and thus does not invite the kind of action Arendt considers so essential. In her review of Ebest's work, E. Shelley Reid maintains that her own experience of teaching the practicum course "constitutes simultaneously the most rewarding and the most frustrating work I've done as a WPA," a view informed audibly by the presence of "new and continuing teachers who do not see composition as their scholarly field, and sometimes do not see teaching as their ultimate goal" (242). The lofty task, then, of creating a collective, of getting graduate students to "buy in" to a shared sense of responsibility for composition in the university, is an enduring challenge. Even Ebest, while advocating for collaborative learning in the practicum course, acknowledges that graduate students may resist group work if it lacks some clear connection to their perceived and immediate needs (121). The following questions remain: On what grounds do graduate students choose to opt in? On what terms, for new graduate students, does the first-year classroom come to occupy, as indistinguishable, teaching and knowledge making, thus cutting off the otherwise inevitable teacher/scholar decision? In *The Human Condition*, Arendt describes the hero's "courage" as "present in a willingness to act and speak at all, to insert one's self into the world and begin a story of one's own" (186). The overarching question we face in our work to prepare and support graduate student teachers is not only how to give them the courage to, as Higgins urges, "write [their] story in pencil" but how to get them to care enough about our world to want to even begin their story here.

While I have largely avoided making specific programmatic suggestions and prefer instead that others take Arendt's concepts and the experiences I explore here and problem-solve in ways that are appropriate to their specific local contexts, I do believe in the importance of facilitating opportunities for graduate students' teaching experiences to foster knowledge making in the context of Arendt's ideas about schooling. This means that their classroom products, their innovations, and their revisions to curricula, materials, and teaching approach be experimental and afforded some due protection from the heavy responsibility of being an ultimate authority or singular example for the first-year students in their classrooms. In part, WPA research on the efficacy of writing center tutoring in training graduate students before their entrance into the first-year classroom suggests one possible means—though the reviews are mixed—of supporting the idea of a mediated space for graduate student learning.[4] Exciting innovations not only to study graduate students' experiences but also to invite them to collaborate as researchers in the field are underway as I write; my hope is that we will continue to see their emerging relevance.[5] An earlier intervention to this end, Tina Lavonne Good and Leanne B. Warshauer's collection, *In Our Own Voice: Graduate Students Teach Writing*, is a practical example of graduate students' reflections on their classroom experiences and adds immeasurably to these goals. Certainly, there are other efforts; my discussion here is not meant to be exhaustive.[6] An accumulating and ever-changing record of graduate students' pedagogical contributions, reflective writing, curricular revisions, and programmatic suggestions could serve the field—from new graduate students themselves to experienced WPAs—as a teaching and research tool.

Just as Arendt has taught me to read graduate students' first classroom experiences as a complex knot of competing and interlocked factors, I have come to see my own role as writer and thinker in this context as equally layered. All great words and deeds depend upon a good storyteller, without which, Arendt tells us, "the story they enact and tell, would not survive at all" (*Human Condition* 173). In this regard, I hope that this project—and my role as storyteller—preserves the stories of four new graduate students in a way that honors their contributions and invites further questioning and sharing. But in this hope for continued conversation, I want to stake out a place for this book, too, in a middle space, on the line between historical record and critical innovation. For the very reason that the stories shared here are not meant to be generalized representations, my goal is to invite an evolving dialogue full of counter-examples, questions, and new or revised applications of these Arendtian concepts to the site of graduate students' first semester classrooms. With this, I hope this book can serve as an example of Arendtian action: an evolving and continuous change of course, a reason to return repeatedly to the role of graduate student teachers in renewing our always-aging world of composition in the university.

I am excited by the prospect of ongoing innovations to better prepare graduate students to teach writing and look forward to these newest teacher/scholars' increased involvement in the discipline of composition, its body of research and its classrooms. My hope is that Arendt's concepts resonate with other researchers, scholars, administrators, and, of course, new graduate student teachers as we all make our way and attempt to "think what we are doing." Laboring always threatens to overtake what we do as compositionists, from our earliest teaching experiences to our furious administrative efforts to make programs work, and thus keeps alive the potential dismissal of composition as mere "service" and continues to hold a deserved valuing of our work at bay. Any among us—would that be all of us?—who fight seemingly endless, uphill battles against colleagues in other disciplines that involve "proving" the legitimacy and rigor of our course proposals, program innovations, and scholarly endeavors understand this tension well. I make this last point fully aware of the difficulties around this step beyond a consuming kind of labor. Arendt asks us to see the relationships between our potential capacities, to think of what we do as multi-part and, consequently, to see that these parts need each other for health and growth. My closing question, then, for our field is this: If it is Arendt's "love of the world" that keeps us, in part, doing what we do in "our" world, how do we show our love? My own response is that we honor beginnings, particularly those of the new graduate student teachers we recruit into our classrooms and our discipline.

APPENDIXES

NOTES

WORKS CITED AND CONSULTED

INDEX

Dear New TA:

Congratulations on your acceptance to Public U and recent teaching assignment! My name is Jessica Restaino, and I am starting my fifth year of doctoral work. I am currently conducting a research study on teacher training in writing instruction. Currently, I am seeking four new TAs to participate in part of my research. Here are the perks:

1. You will be reimbursed $150 toward your book purchases at the end of the semester. This money has been generously donated by Dr. _____, Director of _____.

2. By volunteering, you will also have extra support during your very first semester of teaching. I served two years as a mentor for new TAs and even won the College of Liberal Arts Distinguished Teaching Award this spring. In addition to acting as your assigned mentor, I will be available to you for any extra advice, counsel, or moral support you need—call anytime.

3. Your participation really only requires that you let me talk with you periodically, ask for your insights on your experiences, visit your classroom a couple times, and review some of your students' papers. There will be no additional work for you. I will try hard not to bother you much and, should you show up in my published work, you will be entirely anonymous.

4. This study is not an attempt to show what's "wrong" with our system at Public U; rather, this study is geared toward improving and strengthening all the good stuff we already have

going on. So, your participation is important to our department, and writing programs in general, in terms of helping grad students be better teachers.

The requirements for participation are really pretty simple. If you have never taught writing before and this will be your first semester at Public U (in either the creative writing or PhD program), you qualify. If you're interested, I need to know soon so I can get organized. Please contact me via email at _____ or by phone at _____. I would love to work with you. I'm someone who has been through all levels of the PhD—courses, protocol, exams, etc.—and would be only too happy to answer any questions you have, grad student to grad student.

Please get in touch with me **no later than August 20** if you are interested. First come, first served. I will visit your new teacher orientation to say hello and certainly will stop by the practicum course as well. I look forward to hearing from you soon. Enjoy the rest of your summer!

Take care and many thanks,
Jessica Restaino

APPENDIX B: ORIENTATION SURVEY

Dear _____,

I would like to hear a bit about what you're expecting from English 50, especially now that you have just completed the First-Year Writing Program (FYWP) orientation. I would also like to give you the opportunity to voice any concerns as you approach your first week of teaching. Please take a minute to fill out this form and then just leave it in my mailbox on campus. All data collected as part of this study is confidential and, if published, anonymous. Please drop off this form by the end of the week.

Thanks,
Jessica

FYWP New TA Orientation Evaluation

1. What was the model of writing that you thought the FYWP was presenting to you? How does your picture of the writing process differ from or connect with what FYW is presenting?

2. When was the last time you had direct, explicit instruction in writing?

3. Is there anything that wasn't addressed during orientation that, in your opinion, should have been? In other words, do you feel unprepared in an area you think the orientation could have helped with, but did not?

ON BACK: Optional RANT—I invite you to use the back of this paper to just UNLOAD any worries, questions, concerns, etc., stuff my questions haven't addressed. Of course, you should also feel free to use the back of this paper to expand your responses to Questions 1–3.

NOTES

1. Arendt, Writing Teachers, and Beginnings

1. I am not trying to suggest that there is a complete absence of work on the preparation of graduate students to teach writing, as numerous attempts come to mind (Pytlik and Liggett; Dobrin; Ebest) and are mentioned throughout this book. However, these works deal first with questions of practice, including efforts to put forth "best practices" models for mentoring, practicum courses, and other aspects of graduate students' preparation and support. Ebest's efforts to understand TAs' resistance to teacher training efforts is a notable exception in that she utilizes a number of theoretical lenses in order to explore, especially, the role of gender in shaping graduate students' early initiation into the teaching of writing. Another notable exception is Mary Lou Odom's 2004 dissertation study, which explores graduate students' early interpretations of composition theory.

2. My approach here is informed by Gesa Kirsch and Peter Mortensen's valuable, and enduring, edited collection, *Ethics and Representation in Qualitative Studies of Literacy*, as well as work by Kirsch, Heidi McKee, James Porter, and others on feminist approaches to qualitative research in composition.

3. There exists a range of relevant work on gender and the teaching of first-year composition, far too much to name exhaustively here, but one notable work is Susan Jarratt and Lynn Worsham's collection *Feminism and Composition Studies*. Among other important essays, Eileen Schell's "Costs of Caring" is included in this collection and offers particular insights into the role gender plays in constructing composition teachers' classroom identities. Schell's book *Gypsy Academics and Mother Teachers: Gender, Contingent Labor, and Writing Instruction* explores these tensions more fully and in the context of exploited, contingent faculty.

4. See especially Linda Martín-Alcoff's essay, "The Problem of Speaking for Others."

2. Labor and Endlessness: Necessity and Consumption in the First Semester

1. There are numerous critiques of Arendt's tendency to create a kind of problematic hierarchy among labor, work, and action. See especially Patricia Roberts-Miller's piece "Fighting without Hatred: Hannah Arendt's Agonistic Rhetoric." Such critique is not the central project of Roberts-Miller's work here, but her consideration of the potentially hierarchical nature of these categories for Arendt is useful and situated in the fields of rhetoric and composition.

2. See especially Lad Tobin's introduction, "How the Writing Process Was Born—and Other Conversion Narratives" in Tobin and Newkirk, *Taking Stock: The Writing Process Movement in the '90s.*

3. Among notable exceptions, see Catherine Prendergast's article "Catching Up With Professor Nate: The Problem with Sociolinguistics in Composition Research," which offers a salient critique of an earlier study (by Carol Berkenkotter, Thomas N. Huckin, and John Ackerman) that explores a graduate student's early introduction to the rhetorical culture of writing research. See also the essays featured in Pytlik and Liggett's *Preparing College Teachers of Writing.*

4. For a useful discussion of a positive mentoring relationship between experienced and new TAs, see especially Wanda Martin and Charles Paine's "Mentors, Models, and Agents of Change: Veteran TAs Preparing Teachers of Writing."

5. See especially Bonnie Honig's collection *Feminist Interpretations of Hannah Arendt* for thorough discussion of such critiques.

6. See http://www.wisegeek.com/what-is-an-undertow.htm.

7. Arendt's distinction between "who" and "what," with particular emphasis on its relevance to gender and—perhaps most important—its functioning in her famous work *The Human Condition*, is explored with great insight in Hanna Fenichel Pitkin's *Attack of the Blob: Hannah Arendt's Concept of the Social.*

3. Teachers-as-Students: Work and Action in the Middle Space

1. This is the core of Arendt's fraught argument against school desegregation in her essay "Reflections on Little Rock"; it was not that Arendt opposed school desegregation per se but that she opposed what she saw as the practice of asking children to participate in the adult political arena. Still, much important critical work exists on this controversial essay; see especially Seyla Benhabib's *The Reluctant Modernism of Hannah Arendt.*

2. In fact, Nancy's concerns about grammar instruction tap into existing, though older, debates about the usefulness of grammar instruction, as well as into the contentious issue of skills-based instruction for students who fall outside of what Lisa Delpit has famously called the "culture of power."

3. Such a concept is being explored and experimented with at a number of institutions, though it remains difficult to do well and is still a kind of minority practice. For a valuable discussion of revisions to the practicum course, see especially Sid Dobrin's collection *Don't Call It That: The Composition Practicum*.

4. Although different from Shirley's conference-based, "interactive grading" approach, "contract grading" does ask that student and teacher enter into a written agreement over grading. The practice has gotten much attention from scholars such as Peter Elbow, Ira Shor, and others. However, Shirley had no exposure to this scholarship when she came up with her idea of interactive grading.

5. Anjel's concerns hint strongly of Maxine Hairston's valuable essay "On Not Being a Composition Slave." However, he was not exposed to this piece prior to writing about the "grading machine."

6. The difficulties of translation—moving from theory to practice in the teaching of writing—have been explored widely; see especially Joseph Harris's essay "The Rhetoric of Theory" and Stanley Fish's work in literary criticism, especially *Is There a Text in this Class? The Authority of Interpretive Communities*, as well as Lisa Ede's *Situating Composition: Comp Studies and the Politics of Location*.

7. See especially Richard Wolin's critique, *Heidegger's Children: Hannah Arendt, Karl Löwith, Hans Jonas, and Herbert Marcuse*.

4. Thinking What We Are Doing: Knowledge Making in the Trenches

1. For example, at the 2009 Conference on College Composition and Communication, faculty and graduate students (Ann Updike, Bre Garrett, and Aurora Matzke) from Miami University discussed, in their talk "How Teachers Rise: An Archival and Person-Based Study of the Performative Construction of TA Identity," the successes and failures of their compilation of a master "book" that catalogued TAs' best practices, lesson plans, syllabi, and assignments.

2. For diverse and engaging perspectives on the possibilities of mentoring, including the mentoring of graduate students, see especially Michelle F. Eble and Lyneé Lewis Gaillet's collection *Stories of Mentoring: Theories and Praxis*.

3. For an insightful discussion of Arendt's use (or misuse) of the term "social," see Hanna Fenichel Pitkin's *Attack of the Blob: Hannah Arendt's Concept of the Social.*

4. See especially Melissa Ianetta, Michael McCamley, and Catherine Quick's "Taking Stock: Surveying the Relationship of the Writing Center and TA Training."

5. The most recent I've encountered—which I cited previously—is the efforts of graduate students and faculty at Miami University to compile and use a master "book" of their TAs' contributions to teaching writing, which is then used a resource for teacher preparation.

6. See especially Richard H. Haswell and Min-Zhan Lu's *Comp Tales* and Anne Bramblett and Allison Knoblauch's *What to Expect When You're Expected to Teach: The Anxious Craft of Teaching Composition.*

WORKS CITED AND CONSULTED

While entries for multiple works by the same author or authors are arranged alphabetically by title, those related to the four study participants (Anjel, Nancy, Shirley, and Tess) are arranged chronologically.

Achebe, Chinua. "Dead Man's Path." *Literature: An Introduction to Fiction, Poetry, and Drama.* Ed. X. J. Kennedy and Dana Gioia. 9th ed. New York: Longman, 2005. 382–85. Print.

Anjel. Post-orientation survey. 25 Aug. 2003. Unpublished.

———. Practicum final paper. Dec. 2003. Unpublished.

———. Exit interview. 11 Dec. 2003. Unpublished.

———. Message to the author. 14 Jan. 2004. Email.

Arendt, Hannah. *Between Past and Future: Eight Exercises in Political Thought.* Rev. ed. New York: Viking, 1968. Print.

———. "The Crisis in Education." *Between Past and Future: Eight Exercises in Political Thought.* Rev. ed. New York: Viking, 1968. 173–96. Print.

———. *Eichmann in Jerusalem: A Report on the Banality of Evil.* Rev. ed. New York: Viking, 1965. Print.

———. *Essays in Understanding: 1930–1954.* Ed. Jerome Kohn. New York: Harcourt Brace, 1994. Print.

———. *The Human Condition.* Chicago: U of Chicago P, 1958. Print.

———. *On Revolution.* Rev. 2nd ed. New York: Viking, 1965. Print.

———. "Reflections on Little Rock." *Dissent* 6.1 (Winter 1959): 45–56. Print.

———. "Remarks." Keynote address. American Society of Christian Ethics Conference. Richmond, VA. 1973. Print.

Barry, James D. "Training Graduate Students as Teachers: At Loyola University." *College Composition and Communication* 14 (1963): 74–78. Print.

Bartholomae, David. "Inventing the University." *When a Writer Can't Write: Studies in Writer's Block and Composing Process Problems.* Ed. Mike Rose. New York: Guilford, 1985. 134–65. Print.

———. "The Tidy House: Basic Writing in the American Curriculum." *Journal of Basic Writing* 12.1 (1993): 4–21. Print.

Benhabib, Seyla. *The Reluctant Modernism of Hannah Arendt.* 1996. Lanham: Rowman and Littlefield, 2003. Print.

Berkenkotter, Carol, Thomas N. Huckin, and John Ackerman. "Social Context and Socially Constructed Texts: The Initiation of a Graduate Student into a Writing Research Community." *Landmark Essays on Writing Across the Curriculum.* Ed. Charles Bazerman and David R. Russell. Davis, CA: Hermagoras, 1994. 211–32. Print.

Berthoff, Ann E. *The Making of Meaning: Metaphors, Models, and Maxims for Writing Teachers.* Montclair, NJ: Boynton/Cook, 1981. Print.

Bousquet, Marc. "Composition as Management Science." *Tenured Bosses and Disposable Teachers: Writing Instruction in the Managed University.* Ed. Marc Bousquet, Tony Scott, and Leo Parascondola. Carbondale: Southern Illinois UP, 2004. 11–35. Print.

Bowman, John S. "Training Graduate Students as Teachers: At Pennsylvania State University." *College Composition and Communication* 14 (1963): 73–75. Print.

Bramblett, Anne, and Allison Knoblauch, eds. *What to Expect When You're Expected to Teach: The Anxious Craft of Teaching Composition.* Portsmouth, NH: Boynton/Cook, 2002. Print.

Bridges, Charles W., ed. *Training the New Teacher of College Composition.* Urbana, IL: NCTE, 1986. Print.

Brightman, Carol, ed. *Between Friends: The Correspondence of Hannah Arendt and Mary McCarthy.* New York: Harcourt Brace, 1995. Print.

Canovan, Margaret. *Hannah Arendt: A Reinterpretation of Her Political Thought.* Cambridge, NY: Cambridge UP, 1992. Print.

Crowley, Sharon. *Composition in the University: Historical and Polemical Essays.* Pittsburgh: U of Pittsburgh P, 1998. Print.

Davis, Ken. Rev. of *Training the New Teacher of College Composition. College Composition and Communication* 38 (1987): 219–20. Print.

Delpit, Lisa. "The Silenced Dialogue: Power and Pedagogy in Educating Other People's Children." *Cross-Talk in Comp Theory.* Ed. Victor Villanueva. Urbana, IL: NCTE, 1997. 565–88. Print.

Dobrin, Sidney, ed. *Don't Call It That: The Composition Practicum.* Urbana, IL: NCTE, 2005. Print.

Donovan, Timothy R., Patricia Sprouse, and Patricia Williams. "How TAs Teach Themselves." *Training the New Teacher of College Composition.* Ed. Charles W. Bridges. Urbana, IL: NCTE, 1986. 132–57. Print.

Durst, Russell K. *Collision Course: Conflict, Negotiation, and Learning in College Composition.* Urbana, IL: NCTE, 1999. Print.

Ebest, Sally Barr. *Changing the Way We Teach: Writing and Resistance in the Training of Teaching Assistants.* Carbondale: Southern Illinois UP, 2005. Print.

Eble, Michelle F., and Lyneé Lewis Gaillet, eds. *Stories of Mentoring: Theories and Praxis.* West Lafayette, IN: Parlor, 2008. Print.

Ede, Lisa. "Reading the Writing Process." *Taking Stock: The Writing Process Movement in the '90s.* Ed. Lad Tobin and Thomas Newkirk. Portsmouth, NH: Boynton/Cook, 1994. 31–43. Print.

———. *Situating Composition: Comp Studies and the Politics of Location.* Carbondale: Southern Illinois UP, 2004. Print.

Elbow, Peter. *Writing Without Teachers.* New York: Oxford UP, 1973. Print.

Emig, Janet. *Components of the Composing Process of Twelfth-Grade Writers.* Ann Arbor: University Microfilms, 1970. Print.

Ferrell, Wilfred A. "Training Graduate Students as Teachers: At Arizona State University." *College Composition and Communication* 14 (1963): 78–80. Print.

Ferry, Christopher. "Knowledge Work, Teaching Work, and Doing Composition." *Tenured Bosses and Disposable Teachers: Writing Instruction in the Managed University.* Ed. Marc Bousquet, Tony Scott, and Leo Parascondola. Carbondale: Southern Illinois UP, 2004. 242–49. Print.

Fish, Stanley. *Is There a Text in This Class? The Authority of Interpretive Communities.* Cambridge: Harvard UP, 1980. Print.

Flower, Linda, and John R. Hayes. "A Cognitive Process Theory of Writing." *College Composition and Communication* 31 (1980): 365–87. Print.

Freire, Paulo. *Pedagogy of the Oppressed.* New York: Continuum, 1993. Print.

Gere, Anne Ruggles, and Aaron Schutz. "Service Learning and English Studies: Rethinking 'Public Service.'" *College English* 60 (Feb. 1998): 129–49. Print.

———. "Teaching Writing Teachers." *College English* 47 (1985): 58–65. Print.

Glenn, Cheryl. *Unspoken: A Rhetoric of Silence.* Carbondale: Southern Illinois UP, 2004. Print.

Good, Tina Lavonne, and Leanne B. Warshauer, eds. *In Our Own Voice: Graduate Students Teach Writing.* Boston: Allyn and Bacon, 2000. Print.

Gramsci, Antonio. *Prison Notebooks.* New York: Columbia UP, 1975. Print.

Hairston, Maxine. "Different Products, Different Processes: A Theory about Writing." *College Composition and Communication* 37 (1986): 442–52. Print.

———. "On Not Being a Composition Slave." *Training the New Teacher of College Composition.* Ed. Charles W. Bridges. Urbana, IL: NCTE, 1986. 117–24. Print.

Harrington, Susanmarie, and Tere Molinder Hogue. "The Role of Product in Process: An Approach to Grading and Teacher Response." *English in Texas* 28.2 (1997): 52–60. Print.

Harris, Joseph. "Meet the New Boss, Same as the Old Boss: Class Consciousness in Composition." *College Composition and Communication* 52 (2000): 43–68. Print.

———. "The Rhetoric of Theory." *Writing Theory and Critical Theory.* Ed. John Clifford and John Schilb. New York: MLA, 1994. 141–47. Print.

———. *A Teaching Subject: Composition since 1966.* Upper Saddle River, NJ: Prentice Hall, 1997. Print.

Haswell, Richard H., and Min-Zhan Lu. *Comp Tales: An Introduction to College Composition Through Its Stories.* New York: Longman, 2000. Print.

Hesse, Douglas. "Not Even Joint Custody: Notes from an Ex-WPA." *College Composition and Communication* 56.3 (2005): 501–7. Print.

Higgins, Christopher. "Human Conditions for Teaching: The Place of Pedagogy in Arendt's Vita Activa." *Teachers College Record* 112.2 (2010): 407–45. Print.

Honig, Bonnie, ed. *Feminist Interpretations of Hannah Arendt.* University Park: Pennsylvania State UP, 1995. Print.

hooks, bell. *Teaching to Transgress: Education as the Practice of Freedom.* New York: Routledge, 1994. Print.

Horner, Bruce. "Class, Class Consciousness, and 'Good Teaching Jobs.'" *JAC: A Journal of Composition Theory* 26 (2006): 139–55. Print.

Hull, Glynda. *Changing Work, Changing Workers: Critical Perspectives on Language, Literacy, and Skills.* Albany: State U of New York P, 1997. Print.

Hunting, Robert S. "A Training Course for Teachers of Freshman Composition." *College Composition and Communication* 2 (1951): 3–6. Print.

Ianetta, Melissa, Michael McCamley, and Catherine Quick. "Taking Stock: Surveying the Relationship of the Writing Center and TA Training." *Writing Program Administration* 31: 1–2 (2007). Print.

Jarratt, Susan, and Lynn Worsham, eds. *Feminism and Composition Studies.* New York: MLA, 1998. Print.

Kent, Thomas, ed. *Post-Process Theory: Beyond the Writing-Process Paradigm.* Carbondale: Southern Illinois UP, 1999. Print.

Kirsch, Gesa, and Peter Mortensen. *Ethics and Representation in Qualitative Studies of Literacy.* Urbana, IL: NCTE, 1996. Print.

Kyburz, Bonnie. "Practica, Symposia, and Other Coercive Acts in Composition Studies." *Don't Call It That: The Composition Practicum.* Ed. Sidney Dobrin. Urbana, IL: NCTE, 2005. 67–81. Print.

Larson, Richard. "Staffroom Interchange: Training New Teachers of Composition in the Writing of Comments on Themes." *College Composition and Communication* 17.3 (1966): 152–55. Print.

LeFevre, Karen Burke. *Invention as a Social Act.* Urbana, IL: College Composition and Communication, Studies in Writing and Rhetoric, 1987. Print.

Lu, Min-Zhan, and Bruce Horner. *Representing the Other: Basic Writers and the Teaching of Basic Writing.* Urbana, IL: NCTE, 1999. Print.

Lunsford, Andrea, and Lisa Ede. *Singular Texts/Plural Authors: Perspectives on Collaborative Writing.* Carbondale: Southern Illinois UP, 1990. Print.

Martin, Wanda, and Charles Paine. "Mentors, Models, and Agents of Change: Veteran TAs Preparing Teachers of Writing." *Preparing College Teachers of Writing: Histories, Theories, Programs, Practices.* Ed. Betty P. Pytlik and Sarah Liggett. Oxford: Oxford UP, 2001. Print.

Martín-Alcoff, Linda. "The Problem of Speaking for Others." *Cultural Critique* (Winter 1991): 5–31. Print.

McComiskey, Bruce. *Teaching Writing as a Social Process.* Logan: Utah State UP, 2000. Print.

McKee, Heidi, and James Porter. "The Ethics of Digital Writing Research: A Rhetorical Approach." *College Composition and Communication* 59 (2008): 711–49. Print.

Meeks, Lynn Langer, Joyce Kinkead, Keith VanBezooyan, and Erin Edwards. "Fostering Classroom Civility." *Strategies for Teaching First-Year Composition.* Ed. Duane Roen et al. Urbana, IL: NCTE, 2005. 204–11. Print.

Miller, Susan. *Textual Carnivals: The Politics of Composition.* Carbondale: Southern Illinois UP, 1991. Print.

Moake, Frank B. "Training Graduate Students as Teachers: At the University of Illinois." *College Composition and Communication* 14 (1963): 81–84. Print.

Murray, Donald M. "Teach Writing as a Process Not Product." *Rhetoric and Composition: A Sourcebook for Writing Teachers.* Ed. Richard Graves. Upper Montclair, NJ: Boynton/Cook, 1984. 89–92. Print.

Nancy. Post-orientation survey. 25 Aug. 2003. Unpublished.

———. Author's observation notes. 7 Oct. 2003. Unpublished.

———. Message to the author. 26 Oct. 2003. Email.

———. Message to the author. 1 Nov. 2003. Email.

———. Exit interview. 11 Dec. 2003. Unpublished.

———. Message to the author. 14 Jan. 2004. Email.

Neeley, Stacia Dunn. "'Only connect . . . ': Graduate Instructors Choosing the Margin." *In Our Own Voice: Graduate Students Teach Writing.* Ed. Tina Lavonne Good and Leanne B. Warshauer. Boston: Allyn and Bacon, 2000. 19–27. Print.

Newkirk, Thomas. "The Narrative Roots of Case Study." *Methods and Methodology in Composition Research.* Ed. Gesa Kirsch and Patricia A. Sullivan. Carbondale: Southern Illinois UP, 1992. 130–52. Print.

Noddings, Nel. *Philosophy of Education.* Boulder: Westview, 1995. Print.

Odom, Mary Lou. "Before the Classroom: Teachers Theorizing First-Year Composition Pedagogy." Diss. U of Wisconsin–Madison, 2004. Print.

Olson, Gary. "Toward a Post-Process Composition: Abandoning the Rhetoric of Assertion." *Post-Process Theory: Beyond the Writing-Process Paradigm.* Ed. Thomas Kent. Carbondale: Southern Illinois UP, 1999. 7–15. Print.

Perl, Sondra. "The Composing Process of Unskilled Writers at the College Level." *Research in the Teaching of English* 13 (1979): 317–36. Print.

Pitkin, Hanna Fenichel. *The Attack of the Blob: Hannah Arendt's Concept of the Social.* Chicago: U of Chicago P, 1998. Print.

Pratt, Mary Louise. "Arts of the Contact Zone." *Profession 91.* New York: MLA, 1991. 33–40. Print.

Prendergast, Catherine. "Catching up with Professor Nate: The Problem with Sociolinguistics in Composition Research." *JAC: A Journal of Composition Theory* 17.21 (1997): 39–52. Print.

Prichard, Nancy S. "The Training of Junior College English Teachers." *College Composition and Communication* 21 (1970): 48–54. Print.

Pytlik, Betty P., and Sarah Liggett. *Preparing College Teachers of Writing: Histories, Theories, Programs, Practices.* Oxford: Oxford UP, 2001. Print.

Reid, E. Shelley. "Anxiety of Influencers: Composition Pedagogy in the 21st Century." Rev. of *Changing the Way We Teach: Writing and Resistance in the Training of Teaching Assistants,* by Sally Barr Ebest. *WPA Journal* 31 (Fall/Winter 2007): 1–2, 241–49. Print.

Roberts, Charles. "A Course for Training Rhetoric Teachers at the University of Illinois." *College Composition and Communication* 6 (1955): 190–94. Print.

Roberts-Miller, Patricia. "Fighting without Hatred: Hannah Arendt's Agonistic Rhetoric." *Journal of Advanced Composition* 22.3 (2002): 585–601. Print.

Roen, Duane, Lauren Yena, Veronica Pantoja, Eric Waggoner, and Susan K. Miller, eds. *Strategies for Teaching First-Year Composition.* Urbana, IL: NCTE, 2005. Print.

Ruszkiewicz, John J. "Training New Teachers Is a Process." *College Composition and Communication* 38 (1987): 461–64. Print.

Schell, Eileen. "The Costs of Caring: 'Feminism' and Contingent Women Workers in Composition Studies." *Feminism and Composition*. Ed. Lynn Worsham and Susan Jarratt. New York: MLA, 1998. 74–93. Print.

———. *Gypsy Academics and Mother Teachers: Gender, Contingent Labor, and Writing Instruction*. Portsmouth, NH: Heinemann-Boynton/Cook, 1998. Print.

Schwartz, Joseph. "One Method of Training the Composition Teacher." *College Composition and Communication* 6 (1955): 200–204. Print.

Shaughnessy, Mina. *Errors and Expectations: A Guide for Teachers of Basic Writing*. New York: Oxford UP, 1977. Print.

Shirley. Post-orientation survey. 25 Aug. 2003. Unpublished.

———. Message to the author. 5 Oct. 2003. Email.

———. Message to the author. 11 Oct. 2003. Email.

———. Message to the author. 7 Nov. 2003. Email.

———. Practicum final paper. Dec. 2003. Unpublished.

Shor, Ira. *Empowering Education: Critical Teaching for Social Change*. Chicago: U of Chicago P, 1992. Print.

Sommers, Nancy. "The Case for Research: One Program Administrator's Story." *College Composition and Communication* 56.3 (Feb. 2005): 507–14. Print.

———. "Revision Strategies of Student Writers and Experienced Adult Writers." *College Composition and Communication* 31.4 (1980): 378–88. Print.

Tess. Post-orientation survey. 25 Aug. 2003. Unpublished.

———. Message to the author. 15 Sept. 2003. Email.

———. Message to the author. 20 Sept. 2003. Email.

———. Practicum review paper. 22 Sept. 2003. Unpublished.

———. Message to the author. 1 Oct. 2003. Email.

———. Message to the author. 7 Oct. 2003. Email.

———. Message to the author. 17 Oct. 2003. Email.

———. Message to the author. 29 Oct. 2003. Email.

———. Message to the author. 17 Nov. 2003. Email.

———. Message to the author. 26 Nov. 2003. Email.

———. Message to the author. 4 Dec. 2003. Email.

———. Message to the author. 7 Dec. 2003. Email.

Tobin, Lad. "How the Writing Process Was Born—and Other Conversion Narratives." *Taking Stock: The Writing Process Movement in the '90s*. Ed. Lad Tobin and Thomas Newkirk. Portsmouth, NH: Boynton/Cook, 1994. 1–16. Print.

Tobin, Lad, and Thomas Newkirk, eds. *Taking Stock: The Writing Process Movement in the '90s*. Portsmouth, NH: Boynton/Cook, 1994. Print.

Updike, Ann, Bre Garrett, and Aurora Matzke. "How Teachers Rise: An Archival and Person-Based Study of the Performative Construction of TA Identity." Conference on College Composition and Communication. San Francisco, CA. Mar. 2009. Conference paper.

Williams, Raymond. *Keywords: Vocabulary of Culture and Society.* New York: Oxford UP, 1985. Print.

Wolin, Richard. *Heidegger's Children: Hannah Arendt, Karl Löwith, Hans Jonas, and Herbert Marcuse.* Princeton: Princeton UP, 2003. Print.

Workshop Reports. "The Composition/Communication Course in the Teacher-Training Program." *College Composition and Communication* 11 (1960): 159–61. Print.

———. "Teacher-Training for Composition or Communication." *College Composition and Communication* 2 (1951): 31–32. Print.

INDEX

Jessica Restaino is assistant professor of English and associate director of English education at Montclair State University. Her scholarly interests include writing teacher preparation, community-based writing, rhetorics of gender and maternity, and political theory. She has published essays in *Reflections: A Journal of Writing, Service-Learning, and Community Literacy*; *Thirdspace: A Journal of Feminist Theory and Culture*; and *Academic Exchange Quarterly*. With Laurie Cella, she is currently coediting an essay collection that reexamines sustainability in community-based writing work.

CCCC STUDIES IN WRITING & RHETORIC
Edited by Joseph Harris, Duke University

The aim of the CCCC Studies in Writing & Rhetoric (SWR) series is to influence how writing gets taught at the college level. The methods of studies vary from the critical to historical to linguistic to ethnographic, and their authors draw on work in various fields that inform composition—including rhetoric, communication, education, discourse analysis, psychology, cultural studies, and literature. Their focuses are similarly diverse—ranging from individual writers and teachers, to classrooms and communities and curricula, to analyses of the social, political, and material contexts of writing and its teaching. Still, all SWR volumes try in some way to inform the practice of writing students, teachers, or administrators. Their approach is synthetic, their style concise and pointed. Complete manuscripts run from 40,000 to 50,000 words, or about 150–200 pages. Authors should imagine their work in the hands of writing teachers as well as on library shelves.

SWR was one of the first scholarly book series to focus on the teaching of writing. It was established in 1980 by the Conference on College Composition and Communication (CCCC) to promote research in the emerging field of writing studies. Since its inception, the series has been copublished by Southern Illinois University Press. As the field has grown, the research sponsored by SWR has continued to articulate the commitment of CCCC to supporting the work of writing teachers as reflective practitioners and intellectuals. For a list of previous SWR books, see the SWR link on the SIU Press website at www.siupress.com.

We are eager to identify influential work in writing and rhetoric as it emerges. We thus ask authors to send us project proposals that clearly situate their work in the field and show how they aim to redirect our ongoing conversations about writing and its teaching. Proposals should include an overview of the project, a brief annotated table of contents, and a sample chapter. They should not exceed 10,000 words.

To submit a proposal or to contact the series editor, please go to http://uwp.aas.duke.edu/cccc/swr/.

OTHER BOOKS IN THE CCCC STUDIES IN WRITING & RHETORIC SERIES